Praise For *Heart Centered Pregnancy*

MW01040094

Truly, this guided journal asks pregnant people the precise questions to spark intuition, personal growth, and self-love, leading them toward a more informed and intentional birth and parenthood that doesn't hinge on doing it the "right way." There is only "your way," and this journal will help you find out just what that is!

--Brandy Ferner, author, <u>Adult Conversation: A Novel</u>

Nikki Shaheed has created a journal that is not only inclusive and full of knowledge but includes every aspect of birth, from beginning to end and after. This journal is a handheld gift that will be a treasure to any birthing person, especially those looking to step into their next phase of life using reflection and ceremony.

--Sabia Wade, Founder of For The Village and Birthing Advocacy Doula Trainings

Nikki Shaheed's **Heart-Centered Pregnancy Journal** is exactly what parents have been asking me for, and I can't wait to share it with them. She seamlessly weaves the profound depth of the journey of pregnancy, birth, and early parenting into bite-sized moments of reflection and awareness to gradually bring each reader, each participant, through their own unique journey of the heart. A true gem for parents-to-be, and the birth professionals who support them.

--Farrah Sheehan Deselle, MSN, RN, IBCLC, CLC, CCE (BFW)

Reading this book allowed me the grace that I needed to see the journey of the birth of my child as a meaningful journey even when I knew things would not go 'as planned.' It taught me to give myself the space I needed in my own head and heart to silence the unimportant chatter and open myself to the transition into motherhood. I highly recommend this book, as it's an invaluable tool for new and repeat parents who desire to grow in their connection to self, spouse, and child. You won't regret implementing this tool on your journey into motherhood.

--Sekinat Kassim McCormick, MD

If you are looking for a journal to empower you on your pregnancy and birth journey, then this is the journal. The author made the journal easy to read and she provides interactive activities to keep you mindful of all the emotions you experience while becoming a parent. I highly recommend this journal to any new or experienced parent that needs a safe place to process their thoughts and feelings.

--Whitni F. Toson, MA, Licensed Professional Counselor

Nikki Shaheed was my childbirth educator and doula for all three of my children's births, but she did so much more than help me cope with the difficult work of labor and delivery. Through an unplanned cesarean and then two home births, she held my hand, literally and figuratively, so that I came through each experience changed but not shattered. She lit the sometimes shadowy path for my husband and I as new parents, helping us use the experience of birth as an opportunity to grow our relationship closer. Nikki is not only an expert within the realm of childbirth, but she was also my own personal tour guide for surviving Postpartum, and navigating parenthood in a society that's not always set up for our success. The work she is doing, being a fierce guardian of all things surrounding birth and babies, is nothing short of sacred. I believe her journal illuminates some of the aspects of bringing a life into the world not found in any other pregnancy book on the market.

--Shelley Garza, MA, LMFT, LPC

Heart Centered Pregnancy Journal

Cultivating Intuition, Connection, and Resilience for Pregnancy, Birth, and Postpartum

Nikki Shaheed

ISBN 978-1-7334094-1-4
ISBN Kindle 978-1-733409407
ISBN International 978-1-7334094-6-9

Cataloging in Publication Data
Shaheed, Nikki
Heart-Centered Pregnancy Journal: Cultivating Intuition, Connection, and Resilience for Pregnancy, Birth, and Postpartum
Excerpt From *The Velveteen Rabbit* by Margery Williams Bianco courtesy of public domain.
Edited by Andrea Brunner
Cover design and image by Leigh Ann Sharp
Interior chapter illustrations by Nathan Grant

Visit **https://www.nikkishaheed.com**
https://birthingfromwithin.com
nikki@birthingfromwithin.com

Dedicated to my grandmother, Jan Parker, who taught me what it means to do heart-centered work in service to others.

Contents

Lineage

Like many parents, I experienced a shattering after giving birth. Thinking that perhaps I had just followed the wrong formula, I tried a different formula for my second birth and shattered once again. Only through this process of falling apart and piecing myself back together again and again did my soul open enough to hear the song of Birthing From Within.

By the time I gave birth to my third child, I understood that I was inherently worthy of love and support no matter where my baby was born. My years as a Birthing From Within Mentor had solidified this knowing in my bones, so that I was able to birth with more freedom and unattachment to outcome than I had ever imagined.

My births were all so different, and yet the wisdom in this book applies to all of them. It stretches from the operating room where my first child was born, to my bedroom where my third child was born.

This is how I know it must be shared with the world again and again, through the books that have already been published by Birthing From Within founder Pam England, CNM, MA, through this book, and through those that will follow. Parents need inclusive, holistic, and compassionate preparation for birth, regardless of how it unfolds.

My training with Birthing From Within began in 2012 under the mentorship of Virginia Bobro, IBCLC, CCE(BFW), CD(DONA), who blew my mind wide open with her wisdom. Virginia guided me through many meaningful insights and across multiple personal thresholds. I am forever changed because of her guidance.

In 2013, I began also training under Pam England. She taught me that instead of learning the "right" way to birth or mentor parents about birth, I could continue to open and open and open to new possibilities, new insights, new guides, and new ways of being.

Through Pam's own birth trauma, and her process of seeking deep truths about herself and about birth, the expansive and heart-centered philosophy of Birthing From Within was born. Since 1998, parents and birth professionals around the world have been deeply impacted by Pam's teachings through her workshops and books.

You will see Pam's work referenced again and again throughout this journal, as none of this would have been possible without the powerful foundation that she created, and the wise mentoring of both Pam England and Virginia Bobro.

Compass

My vision for this journal is not for you to have a beautiful, preserved artifact of your pregnancy upon completion, although you may find that you enjoy looking back on it after you give birth. I want it to be a place where you can write down your hopes, your fears, your dreams, and your insights.

A journal full of personal excavations and new discoveries has no business being pristine. Don't be afraid to scribble, fray the pages, and crease the spine. Personal growth work is never dainty. It is a messy endeavor with the power to bring both a lightness of heart and a grounded sense of self on the other side.

This journal is a companion to help you find your inner voice, uncover the buried parts of yourself, and celebrate your gestation as a parent. It is a heart-centered field guide, a map for you to navigate your way through birth as a Heroic Journey.[1]

---

[1] Pam England, CNM, MA, *Ancient Map for Modern Birth: Preparation, Passage, and Personal Growth during Your Childbearing Year* (Albuquerque: Seven Gates Media, 2017)

Purpose

Parents often emerge from the birth experience feeling lost – like they were lacking a map to navigate the transformation, uncertainty, and soul opening that would accompany their journey into parenthood. So often, I hear parents who are trying to make sense of their birth experience talk about how the knowledge they had wasn't enough.

While it is important for modern birthing parents to have an understanding of birth and the maternal healthcare system before their baby's arrival, it is also easier than ever to become so overwhelmed by all of the books, blogs, articles, films, and advice that they have a mental shutdown.

In the last few decades, the childbearing year has turned into a time for making decisions, taking tests, assimilating data, and trying to "get it right." Despite the massive amount of knowledge, training, and learning materials available to pregnant people, the rate of birth trauma is steady and consistent.

Deep down on a soul level, a part of you feels that something may be missing from your prenatal preparation. It's not another manual, blog, or documentary. If that type of preparation really filled you up when you were hungry, wouldn't you come to a place of satiation and stop? Is the answer to learn more, or is the answer to look elsewhere to fill yourself with what you need to give birth?

For most pregnant people meditation, creativity, self-reflection, ceremony, and ritual are low on their list of priorities. Tasks designed to help those preparing to give birth move out of their thinking brain and into their intuitive, instinctual mind seem almost inaccessible. Focusing on this type of preparation may even seem self-indulgent.

In a culture that has told you not to trust your body, to silence yourself in order to belong, to trust authority over your own inner voice, and to put others' needs before your own, you need a guide to untangle these complex issues that affect your words, actions, and decisions. You need a way to sort through your beliefs and how they might be limiting you in pregnancy, birth, and postpartum.

This is your opportunity to begin tearing down the limitations that your lifelong conditioning has created. Your journal is a safe space to explore, dream, purge, reflect, and create. It's a way to open doors to the parts of yourself that have been hidden away – the very parts that you may need to access in order to get through the initiation of childbirth.

The work you engage in throughout this journal will help you to listen within. It will take you beyond the external noise, advice, stories, statistics, and dogma so that you can nurture your own intuition and creativity. This journal is an opportunity to unearth your rich inner resources, and excavate the beliefs, thought patterns, and habits that could impact you in pregnancy, birth, and postpartum.

Gathering

Gathering information about birth can be similar to picking berries. As you gather berries in your birth facts basket, a leaf or a bug may land on your pile. Maybe other people even toss some items in your basket. It's not unusual for parents to wind up with so much in their basket that it's difficult or impossible to sort through what is nourishing, and what is not. [2]

As you gather resources to help you feel better prepared for birth, consider how you decide where to look, and how you decide which information to accept and which to reject. You may be drawn only to sweet berries that make you feel good, like positive birth stories. You may devour everything because you're not sure how to discern what is helpful. You may even eat a lot of bitter berries, hoping that they will inoculate you against disappointment.

---

[2] Pam England, CNM, MA, *Ancient Map for Modern Birth: Preparation, Passage, and Personal Growth during Your Childbearing Year* (Albuquerque: Seven Gates Media, 2017)

Journal below about your gathering so far in your pregnancy. What is it that you are drawn to, and why? What are you repelled by, and why?

Mentor

As you embark on a journey of initiation, it's important to find a mentor to offer you guidance and perspective: a wise elder who understands the lay of the *inner* landscape. This mentor may come in the form of a friend, family member, doula, childbirth educator, or birth attendant.

A mature mentor will help you look within to find your own answers and wisdom. They will take a genuine interest in the way you see birth, the world, and yourself. While they may step into the role of teacher at times, their teaching will be tailored to what you bring to the moment instead of serving you a carbon copy of what they taught to all of their other mentees.

Mentors are not cheerleaders. They have the wisdom to know that only filling your belly with sweet berries won't sustain you in the long term. Mentors may give you tasks that bring discomfort or uncertainty. They know that this is the gentle and compassionate way you help you prepare for the bigger initiation you are gearing up for. They will also know when to ease up on you and how to help you celebrate your growth.

Journal below about mentors who are already part of your life, or where you will begin your search for mentors to guide you and honor your journey through the childbearing year.

Hunting

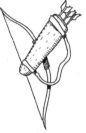

While you will need to gather information about birth physiology, common medical interventions, and the setting in which you plan to give birth, there is more to preparing for birth than gathering data. Rather than looking for the "right" answers and input from others, this kind of learning is an internal excavation known as hunting.[3]

The image of a cheetah is quite different from the berry gatherer. Cheetahs do not lunge at the first prey that wanders by. They don't ask other cheetahs for advice on how to hunt or seek approval on their gazelle-stalking skills. Rather, they wait in a quiet, meditative state until the right moment and then pounce!

When humans are immersed in spiritual hunting, they step away from their everyday busyness. Hunters and Huntresses set down the to-do list, quiet their cell phones, back away from the sink full of dishes, and take time to look inward. This may be a lengthy endeavor, or a matter of taking a few moments for self-reflection.

---

[3] Pam England, CNM, MA, *Ancient Map for Modern Birth: Preparation, Passage, and Personal Growth during Your Childbearing Year* (Albuquerque: Seven Gates Media, 2017)

When you look within at your knowing, your experiences, and your resources, a vast ocean of possibilities is revealed. Endless creativity is within you to access, to open up to, and to help you find new insights and deeper knowing. Instead of asking, "What do I need to know to give birth?" your Hunter/Huntress archetype's questions are more introspective. "What do I already know about coping with pain and intensity? What do I do when I don't know what to do? What is this moment asking of me? Where do my beliefs about birth come from? Which ones are serving me? Which ones are not?"

Hunting within will take you on a journey through your psyche, your belief system, and the many experiences you have lived up until now. It will help you access a deep well of knowledge that you couldn't find in an entire library full of books, and open doors to new ways of being and doing. It will help you navigate your birth experience and come out the other side more emotionally intact, regardless of the specific events of your birth.

Create

"Without leaps of imagination, or dreaming, we lose the excitement of possibilities. Dreaming, after all, is a form of planning." — *Gloria Steinem*

As you take one step at a time through the labyrinth of birth, you will be forging a pathway through the unknown.[4] Your story will unfold from one moment to the next without you knowing what lies around the next bend in the road. Art making is a way to practice being in the present and doing whatever the moment calls for, instead of trying to plan, negotiate, and think your way through the process.[5] It's a way of sensing what to do next, rather than following a prescribed recipe.

---

[4] Pam England, *Labyrinth of Birth* (Santa Barbara, BFW Books, 2010)

[5] Pam England, CNM, MA and Rob Horowitz, PhD, *Birthing From Within: An Extra-Ordinary Guide to Childbirth Preparation* (Albuquerque: Partera Press, 1998)

When you create art, you connect with the symbols that are relevant to you in your birth preparation process. You listen within to decide what should happen next, rather than consulting with outside "experts." Questions, answers, insights, and new learning arise from within when you allow yourself to draw, paint, or sculpt beyond what you already know – beyond what's familiar and comfortable. This is where the art becomes the teacher, the place where the emphasis shifts from the end product to the journey that leads you there.

As you create birth art throughout this journal, allow yourself to keep going until you are surprised, until you have entered the place of uncertainty, and until you have had at least one chance to keep going when you didn't know what to do next. This threshold between the known and the unknown is the opening for new learning. When art is focused on the process rather than the end product, you may find yourself excited, doubtful, irritated, invigorated, or anywhere in between. Keep going anyway, bringing your whole heart to the task at hand. This is practice for labor. This is an opportunity to live with what is, in the present.

Emerald City

In *The Wizard of Oz,* by L. Frank Baum, Dorothy and her companions approach the Gate to the Emerald City and request to see the Wizard. The Gatekeeper allows them to come in, but warns that they must wear special sunglasses to protect them from the blinding brilliance of the Emerald City, which he locks onto their heads. Sure enough, when Dorothy and her friends enter the city, everything is a dazzling emerald color – almost as if by magic. Even Dorothy's dress and Toto's ribbon have transformed to a radiant green.

The Wizard refuses to help them with their wishes until the Wicked Witch is dead, so Dorothy departs the Emerald City and leaves her sunglasses behind at the threshold. As she walks away, Dorothy looks down and sees that once again her dress is plain, and that Toto's ribbon is also the same color it was before. The glasses weren't protecting them from the brilliance of the Emerald City, but rather creating an illusion.

As you move through life, pregnancy, and birth, you see the world through your own "sunglasses" – the lens of conditioning that you were raised with as a child or influenced by as a teen and adult. They color the way you see the world. Your sunglasses create layers of assumptions, bias, and invisible walls within you that keep you in check. These inner barriers may keep you from speaking up, from expressing your emotions, or from listening to your gut. They could make helpful options inaccessible because you have learned that you absolutely cannot or should not do certain things if you want to belong and be worthy.

When you bring attention to your sunglasses, you have more personal freedom. Noticing where old beliefs control your actions like puppet strings allows you to have choices in the places where the current of your conditioning had previously moved you along a pre-determined path.

The sunglasses you wear are influenced by the time you live in, your geographic location, community, religion, education, and family. There are many, many factors that influence the way you see the world, other people, and yourself.

In this journal, you will examine the metaphorical sunglasses that affect you both prenatally and in the birth space. You will bring attention to the origins of your sunglasses, and expose the incomplete truths in the absolute, black-and-white thinking that those sunglasses can create. You will have more freedom to abide in the gray areas, the in-between spaces, the threshold between light and shadow.

Lens

Before you begin, you'll need to gather drawing materials. Chalk pastels are ideal, but work with what you have. Even magic markers or a pen will suffice for your process.

Your beliefs, thoughts, and ideas are represented by symbols extracted from your experiences, your culture, and the influence of people around you. Your feelings about birth are a culmination of everything you've ever heard about birth, babies, parents, hospitals, pain, discomfort, connection, and interacting with authority figures, to name a few.[6]

Every TV show you've watched that included birth, every birth story that you've overheard, and every book you've read represents a part of your collective understanding of birth. Every conversation about birth with friends, family members, and strangers all the way back to childhood impacts the way you see birth now, whether you agree with what was said or not.

---

[6] Pam England, CNM, MA, *Ancient Map for Modern Birth: Preparation, Passage, and Personal Growth during Your Childbearing Year* (Albuquerque: Seven Gates Media, 2017)

On the next page, insert symbols of your early impressions, and more recent impressions of birth. Even if your passive and direct learning about birth from long ago no longer aligns with your current beliefs, include those symbols anyway. Capture every image you can think of, even if those images contradict one another. Each layer of understanding is a piece of your cumulative knowing about childbirth.

Which symbols surprised you in your art making process? If you were to dialogue with those symbols, what might they say to you?

Rest

Our culture is embedded with messaging that glorifies self-sacrifice in the name of productivity. The values of our society are made clear in the way that people talk about hard work as an important virtue, a means of getting ahead and earning respect. This short-sighted fixation on keeping your nose to the grindstone can easily lead to burnout and depletion, especially when you are growing or caring for a new life.

Throughout your pregnancy, your body works hard to fulfill the needs of your baby. This process of creation takes a great deal of energy and resources from your body. It's important to build rest into your day to give yourself an opportunity for restoration. It takes courage to push back against demanding cultural narratives and listen to what your body is communicating to you.

Creating space for naps and relaxation may mean that other tasks need to be set down or delegated. What are you willing to put aside for a while in order to make time for physical and mental restoration? High expectations? Housework? Social commitments?

How will cultivating this practice of prioritizing your rest serve you throughout your pregnancy and the postpartum period?

Nurture

Food has a much deeper meaning than calories, vitamins, and minerals. Every culture has its own unique cuisine and traditions related to food. For some families, sitting down together for dinner is their best opportunity to connect during busy days. For families who deal with food allergies or diabetes, nutrition can become a stressful, calculated ordeal.

Some people connect with others by breaking bread together. Some people share food with sick or stressed loved ones to show they care. Sometimes food is used as a distraction from difficult emotions. Abstaining from certain foods is a way for some to connect to a higher power or support a cause.

What has been your relationship with food as an adult, and as a child? What is the family legacy that has been passed on to you about the meaning and purpose of food? What is serving you well from that narrative? Is there anything you would like to change about your relationship with food during this pregnancy?

Prenatal nutrition is the most effective way for you to influence the health of your pregnancy and baby. The foods you eat now have the potential to prevent diabetes, high blood pressure, and heart disease for your child as an adult.[7]

Through amniotic fluid, your baby can even taste the flavor of the foods you eat. They are already an active participant in your daily eating routine, developing preferences for certain foods in the womb.[8]

When you take stock of your daily nutrition, what is one thing that you're doing well? What is one small change that could make your nutrition a bit more robust?

Remember, this exploration is designed as a tool for self-reflection, not a tool of self-judgment. A heaping tablespoon of self-compassion will be an important ingredient in your daily nutrition routine in order to keep your inner critic from derailing your efforts.

_____

[7] Pam England, CNM, MA, *Ancient Map for Modern Birth: Preparation, Passage, and Personal Growth during Your Childbearing Year* (Albuquerque: Seven Gates Media, 2017)

[8] Pam England, CNM, MA, *Ancient Map for Modern Birth: Preparation, Passage, and Personal Growth during Your Childbearing Year* (Albuquerque: Seven Gates Media, 2017)

Labyrinth

Birthing parents and birth professionals are presented with many "maps" for navigating the journey through Labor Land:

- Friedman's curve, a graph that requires 1-2 cm per hour of dilation for birthing parents
- The hands of a clock
- The three phases of birth – latent, pushing, and expulsion of the placenta
- The graphic showing cervical dilation from one to ten centimeters
- The tracings on a contraction monitor

These maps can give birth attendants and support people a sense of what's happening in the labor, but they don't track the internal experience of the birthing parent and the emotional thresholds they must cross in order to meet their baby.

The labyrinth is an ancient symbol that has been found in China, Ireland, Peru, India, the Southwestern United States, France, and many other places over the span of several thousand years.[9] While these labyrinths can take different shapes and patterns, they all have just one pathway to the center. The path of the labyrinth represents initiation, transformation, and stepping into the unknown, with only one way in and one way out.

---

[9] Pam England, *Labyrinth of Birth* (Santa Barbara, BFW Books, 2010)

As you walk or trace a labyrinth, you may feel the uncertainty and disorientation that are experienced during birth. The twists and turns will take you deeper and deeper inward. There are no wrong turns, no dead ends, and no way to do it wrong. The only task is to keep going, putting one foot in front of the other as you follow the path to the center and back out again.

Use the chart on the next page to help you draw your own labyrinth in the blank space that follows, and then trace your way to the center and back out with your finger. Notice your mind's internal chatter and the emotions that arise for you during this process. Observe how they change, and where you feel them in your body. Journey in and out through the winding passageways seven times, allowing each outward breath to propel you forward along the path.

When your seven tracings are complete, journal about what happened for you as you passed through the unknown again and again. What shifts did you notice in your thoughts? In your body? In your understanding about birth or life?

Crossing the Threshold

The onset of the birth process signifies the crossing of a threshold from everyday life into the alternate reality of Labor Land, from the known to the unknown, from the lived to the not-yet-lived.[10] This time may bring up feelings of excitement, anticipation, or worry. Some people will begin their labor at home, and others may begin their labor in a medical setting with the assistance of technology.

This simultaneous ending of the life you have lived up to this point and the beginning of your life as a parent deserves a ceremonial pause, if only in your mind. This liminal space asks you to ponder – *Here I stand at the threshold of labor. What will be asked of me? What will I have to give up? Am I willing to do it? Who will I become on the other side?*

As you prepare to move through the challenges of labor, what is one word that you would like to hold close to your heart throughout this process? Which attribute would you like to take with you as you walk the path of the unknown?

---

[10] Pam England, CNM, MA and Rob Horowitz, PhD, *Birthing From Within: An Extra-Ordinary Guide to Childbirth Preparation* (Albuquerque: Partera Press, 1998)

Choose one word that you can carry on this journey, whether you find yourself in a forest, your bathtub, a birthing suite, an operating room, or a taxi. Where will you set your inner compass so that you can do the hard work of getting your baby out, with your self-compassion intact?

Make sure that this word isn't one that you will use against yourself later if labor doesn't go as you hope. "Strong" or "powerful" aren't attributes that we can hold in any situation, because sometimes life brings us to our knees in surrender to fate. Instead, explore the attributes behind that word.

What does it mean to be "strong?" Does it mean doing what needs to be done in the moment? Does it mean staying connected to your baby, your labor, your partner, and yourself through whatever may arise? Keep digging until you find the attribute that you want to bring more of into your life, that could be your companion through any kind of birth.

My attribute _____.

Create a threshold space or symbol at the opening of your labyrinth drawing and write your word in or next to that threshold marker. Let it serve as a reminder of the inner shifts that are part of all initiations, and what you will need in order to navigate them.

Don't just write this word down and turn the page, leaving your personal development in the creases of your journal. Practice carrying that word with you through every breath and every step *now*, so that when labor begins your resilience, self-love, flexibility, or whatever other attribute you choose is etched in your heart from weeks or months of practicing.

Carry this word with you through times of joy, pleasure, pain, anger, connection, uncertainty, and doubt. Allow it to become a Heart's Question[11] – How am I bringing this attribute to this moment? This question cannot be answered with words – only action. This is how you will create emotional resilience to weather the highs and lows of labor.

[11] Pam England, CNM, MA, *Ancient Map for Modern Birth: Preparation, Passage, and Personal Growth during Your Childbearing Year* (Albuquerque: Seven Gates Media, 2017)

Mindfulness

Pain is a physical sensation – a message from the body. It is an inevitable part of birth for most people, but suffering is not. Suffering comes from negative mental chatter[12]. It's the story you tell yourself about the pain – that you're not strong enough, that you can't do it, that you should find a way out, or that your situation is hopeless. Suffering takes your intensity and discomfort from challenging to unbearable.

Suffering can only happen in the future – *How much longer will this last? Will pushing be even harder? Will the car ride feel worse than this?* – or in the past – *Why did they ask me all those questions when I was having contractions? I wish I wouldn't have cried in front of the doctor. It was so hard to go through triage!*

By cultivating a practice of mindfulness prenatally, you can reduce suffering in labor[13]. Mindfulness means existing in the present in a state of curiosity, receptivity, and awareness, being present to what is in that moment, without creating a positive or negative story about it. In this state, there is no room left for suffering. There is only what exists in this moment…and this moment…and this moment.

---

[12] Thich Nhat Hanh, *The Miracle of Mindfulness: An Introduction to the Practice of Meditation* (Beacon Press; 1st edition, 1999)

[13] Pam England, CNM, MA and Rob Horowitz, PhD, *Birthing From Within: An Extra-Ordinary Guide to Childbirth Preparation* (Albuquerque: Partera Press, 1998)

Training yourself to live in the present requires practice, intention, and focus. There are many ways to engage in mindfulness, and this practice can be deepened by holding a handful of ice for 1-minute intervals (the length of an average labor contraction) for an "ice contraction." [14] Allow yourself time to rest in between ice contractions, just like in labor. Fully release the sensation of pain to help rewire your mind to uncouple pain from suffering.

Throughout this book, you will find mindfulness practices that can help you develop mental resilience and flexibility, and increase your ability to cope with pain. You may find that some come more naturally than others, or that you like one particular coping practice best. The practice that you like the *least* needs to be practiced twice as often. Practice and practice until it becomes second nature, because working through that which you dislike will help you strengthen your heart and mind like a Samurai preparing for battle.

---

[14] Pam England, CNM, MA and Rob Horowitz, PhD, *Birthing From Within: An Extra-Ordinary Guide to Childbirth Preparation* (Albuquerque: Partera Press, 1998)

Awareness of Breath

The breath is a touchstone that is with you from the moment you emerge from the womb, an old companion whose company you can return to at any time. You can bring awareness to your breath whether it's fast or slow, deep or shallow, loud or soft, noticing the subtle shifts that happen from one breath to the next with a sense of curiosity.

As you draw your attention to your breath, tune in to the way it feels as it moves through your body. Does your belly expand on the inward breath and release on the outward breath? What happens in the space between your inhale and exhale? Does your outward breath make a sound? Does it come from your nose or your lips?

Allow each outward breath to bring more and more focus to your exhale. There's no need to try to slow your breath down or change it in any way. You're simply observing, without judgment, what your breath is doing from one moment to the next. Set your journal down and continue this practice, staying with your breath…

~

Once you have digested this practice, try adding a handful of ice cubes for one-minute "ice contractions," remaining focused on your breath until it's time for the next ice contraction.

You might begin to layer the practice of breath awareness with imagery, like visualizing the ocean tide coming and going with your inward and outward breath. You might also associate a color with releasing, thinking of blowing that color between your lips on your exhale.

Be careful not to jump to these images seeking a "distraction." First, focus your mind through the breath. Then the visuals can arise spontaneously. To distract your mind is to weigh it down with avoidance. To focus your mind is to lighten the burden of suffering chatter.

Ritual and Ceremony

Throughout each day, you cross thresholds without even noticing. You cross the threshold from waking to sleeping. From the bed to the floor. From hungry to satiated. From indoors to outdoors. From partner to employee to friend to consumer to lover.

You have crossed many significant thresholds throughout your life: kindergarten, puberty, first kiss, graduation, pregnancy, and more. Sometimes these thresholds are honored ceremoniously. Other times, they pass with only retrospective appreciation for the fact that you were moving through a liminal space between who you had been and who you would become.

Throughout history, thresholds have traditionally been marked with ritual and ceremony – from baptisms to bat mitzvahs to quinceañeras to wedding receptions and funerals. Formal acknowledgment of these thresholds within a family or community helps ground people who are finding their way through changes to their identity. Ceremony brings awareness to what is being entered into, and what is being left behind.

In western culture, some of these threshold markers have been lost to our modern lifestyle. In our busy lives, we have lost touch with the importance of pausing at thresholds to consider the path that lies ahead. We've lost the art of creating spaces for elders to mentor new initiates in preparation for their journey.

Marking a sacred space to acknowledge stepping into a new identity allows your psyche to recognize that yes, this simultaneous ending and beginning matters. When this ceremony involves community, wise and caring people in your circle can witness you, hold you, and support you as you move from one phase of life into another.

When in your life have you experienced the power of ceremony? A wedding? Graduation? Religious rites? How did this ceremonial acknowledgment of your changing identity impact you on a personal level? If other people were involved in this ceremony, what was it like to have them witness and support you through your journey?

1st Trimester Ceremony

Many parents breathe a sigh of relief as the first trimester comes to an end. It's likely that this milestone will bring relief from any remaining nausea, and that you will soon have more energy as well.

In celebration of this threshold, consider creating a centerpiece with…

- An item from nature representing the natural season you're in (fall leaves, spring blossoms, etc.)
- A candle
- Any special artifacts you've gathered during your transition into pregnancy. It might be your pregnancy test, ginger candies, or saltines.

Perhaps you've even picked up something to enjoy as your belly grows, like a cute top with room to grow that you found at the consignment store, or the comfy pregnancy leggings that a friend lent to you. There may be symbols that represent this time in your life. An apple for fertility. A lemon that's about the same size as your baby. A 3-leaf clover with a leaf for each member of your family, or another plant if you're expecting a second or subsequent baby.

Sit by your centerpiece and take time to journal about your experience of the first trimester:

When did you find out you were pregnant?

How did you feel?

What was your partner's response?

Who did you share the news with?

What changed for you during the last three months?

How did you cope with the challenges that the first trimester brought?

When you feel tired, sick, or depleted, how did you show yourself gentleness?

What are your hopes for the second trimester?

What is one small thing that you would like to do in order to move through your second trimester with intention? Is there a daily mindfulness or movement practice you'd like to begin? Are there nutrition adjustments you would like to make during this time? Something else you're hoping to shift? Allow these intentions to become a sweet invitation to a more centered way of interacting with yourself, rather than a "should" or a rigid to-do list.

If there are people you've been waiting to share the news of your pregnancy with, you may want to include them in your ceremony. You could ask them each to bring a candle for your altar and say a blessing for you, your baby, and your family as they light it.

You could ask them to share what they found most exciting about pregnancy, or how they dealt with the challenges of growing a new life. You could even write these questions on note cards and give one to each person you invite in order to keep this ceremony focused, mindful, and supportive. You can also talk to friends or family members about these questions later if this doesn't feel like the right time to share your pregnancy.

Write down any insights or memories that you would like to hold onto from your First Trimester Ceremony.

Patient or Parent Archetype

The healthcare system does a great job of cultivating the Patient archetype[15] from childhood through adulthood – fostering compliance to maintain the efficiency of the system. This is not an indictment of doctors, nurses, or midwives, but rather an observation of the conditions that the system has created in its own self-interests. When patients don't put up too much resistance, ask too many questions, or assert too much agency, the healthcare system flows smoothly.

This system has many ways of grooming the Patient archetype. Having people take their clothes off or scheduling appointments to only last a few minutes creates an imbalance in power. This dynamic leaves patients in a vulnerable position where they are more likely to yield to the medical professional.

---

[15] Pam England, CNM, MA, *Ancient Map for Modern Birth: Preparation, Passage, and Personal Growth during Your Childbearing Year* (Albuquerque: Seven Gates Media, 2017)

Throughout your pregnancy, you will be gestating a different kind of archetype – the Parent.[16] This archetype is a caretaker of your growing baby and also yourself. While the Patient archetype takes the actions necessary to avoid conflict and helplessness, your Parent archetype knows that there is a time to flow with the system and a time to push back. This part of you is not attached to being liked, making people happy, or heedlessly following someone else's ideology about birth – whether they're from the medical model or "natural birth" model.

Rather, your inner Parent has the discernment and self-love to examine whether a piece of the medical establishment is working for or against you. Your Parent archetype is learning each day to find its voice, on behalf of you, your baby, and your family. Developing this archetype is a process, just like growing a baby. Grant yourself grace for the time it takes your Patient archetype to step back and allow your Parent archetype to bloom.

What do you notice about your conditioning as a Patient? What are the accepted behaviors that you have learned as a Patient? Which behaviors have you learned to put away during the times when you're interacting with the healthcare system?

---

[16] Pam England, CNM, MA, *Ancient Map for Modern Birth: Preparation, Passage, and Personal Growth during Your Childbearing Year* (Albuquerque: Seven Gates Media, 2017)

What differentiates your inner Parent from your inner Patient? What have you already noticed about your gestating Parent archetype? Which qualities would you still like to cultivate in your interactions with the healthcare system as you work to gently untangle years of conditioning?

Wisdom

There is a myth in our modern birth culture: If you learn enough, you can avoid hardship and disappointment. It's true that the knowledge you glean from others may help you avoid common stumbling blocks, but it is unrealistic to think that if you learn enough, you won't get your sneakers dirty on your Heroic Journey.

It is very natural to want to drink from the fountain of knowledge and absorb as much as you can from those who are initiated, who have walked the path that you are getting ready to embark upon. Throughout history, people have sought counsel from wise elders before a life transition in hopes of accessing some of their mentor's far-seeing perspective, gaining a deeper understanding of what they may encounter, and learning how they might overcome challenges on their journey.

Knowledge comes from books, experts, and advisors, but wisdom is cultivated through experience. It's a knowing in your bones rather than a knowing in your head. Wisdom cannot be acquired without struggle. It is essential for a person to be challenged in a way that makes them question what they believed was right, or who they believed they were, in order to unwrap the gift of wisdom.

When examining the difference between knowledge and wisdom, I always think of this beloved passage from *The Velveteen Rabbit*:

"Real isn't how you are made," said the Skin Horse. "It's a thing that happens to you. When a child loves you for a long, long time, not just to play with, but REALLY loves you, then you become Real."

"Does it hurt?" asked the Rabbit.

"Sometimes," said the Skin Horse, for he was always truthful. "When you are Real you don't mind being hurt."

"Does it happen all at once, like being wound up," he asked, "or bit by bit?"

"It doesn't happen all at once," said the Skin Horse. "You become. It takes a long time. That's why it doesn't happen often to people who break easily, or have sharp edges, or have been carefully kept. Generally, by the time you are Real, most of your hair has been loved off, and your eyes drop out and you get loose in the joints and very shabby. But these things don't matter at all, because once you are Real you can't be ugly, except to people who don't understand."

While it's important to become informed about birth and the healthcare system, it is not your job to have all the answers before birth begins. The most important things you will learn through this process will come from meeting the unknown and somehow finding your way through.

Journal about an experience in your life that took you from knowledge to wisdom. What shifted within you at that time? What was given up, or taken? What was gained?

Fulcrum

When you sit at one end of a seesaw, the other side abruptly springs upward. The same is true if you switch sides. However, in the very center – the fulcrum – there is balance, and both sides are within reach.

The birth options presented to expecting parents are often dichotomous; one way is good, and the other way is bad. You're either on the right team or the wrong team, and it seems that most people choose a team either based on what has always been done or in direct opposition to it. This dualistic thinking leaves little room for nuance, for complexity, or for grace.

It's both normal and appropriate to have a goal or work hard for the kind of birth you desire. When that goal can also encompass putting all options, words, and behaviors within the realm of possibility – something you could allow yourself to do if the moment called for it – you create a wider reach for self-compassion.

This is different from saying, "Of course I would do it if it were medically necessary." Unfortunately, "medically necessary" is often an ambiguous term. Birth attendants interpret the needs of a birthing parent and baby based on their own experiences, beliefs, learning, systems they operate within, and basic needs – just like you. Making these judgment calls is more of an art than a litmus test, which can often leave parents feeling confused about whether or not the things that happened during their birth really needed to.

Barring an emergency, there won't be easy answers in birth to determine what is medically necessary or not. For this reason, it is important to tune into your own spectrum of beliefs and work on taking small steps toward the fulcrum prenatally. This will help you take action from a more open and mindful place, rather than rolling to either the passive end or rigid end of the seesaw.

True freedom comes from a commitment to self, even if the very thing you don't want to happen, does. True freedom comes from examining the roots of your beliefs and acknowledging the places where your thoughts and beliefs trend toward dualism, so that you can explore how to move just one notch closer to the fulcrum.

Bring to mind one birth-related topic you feel strongly about, whether it has to do with location, provider, medicine, postpartum adjustment, infant feeding, birth plan, or something else. How do you know to feel so strongly about this topic? What informs your opinion on this topic?

If something came up in birth that caused you to do the thing you don't want to do, or not do the thing you really want to do, having an idea of how you might cope would serve as an emotional safety net. Like holding a cup in each hand, you could feel frustration and disappointment while simultaneously coping. Under these circumstances, a resilient mindset would help you stay focused on showing up for yourself and doing the next best thing, instead of spiraling into self-judgment and despair.

One small thing I could do to cope with this undesired circumstance would be:

Taking one small step toward the fulcrum of my beliefs on this topic would make a difference for me in this way now, and in birth:

One other small thing I could do to cope would be:

Making this commitment to yourself doesn't mean you have to give up your strong feelings about birth. It does, however, give you more breathing room to do what needs to be done in labor, working with the hand that's dealt to you, without attaching your self-worth to a medical outcome.

Centering

*"To think in terms of either pessimism or optimism oversimplifies the truth.
The problem is to see reality as it is." — Thich Nhat Hahn*

If you are attached to a particular way of getting through birth pain, you may feel that you can't make it through without that person or thing. Without it, you may suffer and think that you can't go on. We see this when someone who was attached to their birth ball must remain in the hospital bed, or when a person who planned to birth with an epidural has a labor that moves too fast to administer one.

While it's understandable that you might feel attached to your birth partner's support, it's also helpful to have the inner resources to cope without your birth partner present. At some point during labor, they will need to use the bathroom, eat, or drink. Having a flexible mindset will help you cope while your partner is out of reach, instead of suffering in their absence.

When you are in avoidance, you expend a great deal of energy resisting the object, person, or concept you find undesirable. Your focus settles on an image of what you don't want, rather than moving toward more of what you *do* want. Avoidance can also cause suffering – especially since it rarely resolves the issue you're trying to avoid. It may even fester and grow bigger.

Expending energy on loathing a beeping monitor, the garbage truck emptying a dumpster outside the birth center, or the barking dogs down the street drains energy that you need for coping. Of course, you could ask someone to turn down the volume on a monitor, or request that a neighbor bring their pets inside, but some stimuli cannot be controlled and must, instead, be coped with.

There is a space between attachment and avoidance called awareness. When you are in a state of awareness, you are fully present to what is happening right now. You are observing what is, in this very moment, without judging, trying to control, or needing to change it. You are being with what is, without creating a story about it. It's not good, it's not bad. It just is.

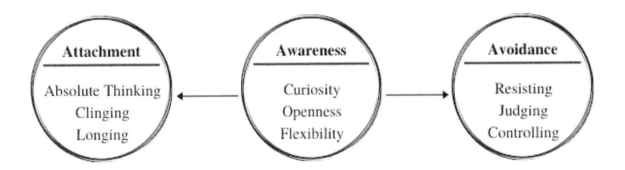

Focused Awareness

When the ticking clock in the delivery room is bad, and the warm water in the shower is good, the mind is busy assessing, categorizing, and even criticizing what is happening around it. The stimuli that are deemed as "negative" become something to avoid, and the mental energy it takes to resist them depletes the energy you have to focus on working through contractions. That resistance can lead to suffering.

By the same token, the stimuli that have been designated as "positive" can cause you to feel attached to them, like you can't cope through contractions without the constant presence of that object, visual, sound, or person.

By developing a non-judgmental mindset about the sensations around you, you can notice what is happening in your environment right now with curiosity. There is no need to create a story or mentally catalog what is "good" or "bad." Without attachment to or avoidance of certain stimuli, you can settle into the open space of awareness.

Try allowing the people and objects in your environment to enter into your consciousness as if you are experiencing them for the first time. Notice what you are seeing, hearing, touching, and your breath.[17] Let these stimuli pass into and out of your awareness without drifting into avoidance or attachment, like steering a ship safely between two islands.

What begins to shift when a blossoming flower, a sputtering muffler, a sensual caress, or a choir of cicadas does not ask for your avoidance or attachment? What happens within you when each sensation is neither good nor bad, it just *is*?

When you have familiarized yourself with this practice, try the one minute "ice contraction" technique. Immediately, the ice will offer you an opportunity to notice physical sensation without running away or forming a narrative about it. You might notice the way the ice yields to the warmth of your hand, or the way it aches in your palm.

These things are not good or bad, they are simply events, moments in time, passing like cars on a highway. Once you have acknowledged the sensation of the ice without resistance, you can notice what else enters your field of consciousness – sights, sounds, other physical sensations – in a grounded state of awareness, openness, and curiosity.

---

[17] Pam England, CNM, MA, *Ancient Map for Modern Birth: Preparation, Passage, and Personal Growth during Your Childbearing Year* (Albuquerque: Seven Gates Media, 2017)

Intention

"You have to take risks. We will only understand the miracle of life fully when we allow the unexpected to happen." — Paulo Coelho

Have you noticed yourself saying, "I'm just going to let whatever happens, happen," as a way to avoid deciding or speaking about what you really hope for in birth? This approach is often used as a strategy to avoid feeling disappointment if the birth takes an unwished-for turn.

Knowing that you may need to make an unexpected stop or change your route doesn't stop you from setting your GPS on a road trip. There is a balance in knowing the value of having a sense of direction and holding the truth that there is more than one way to get to your destination.

Disappointment in a medical or emotional outcome will not be avoided by steering away from thinking about what you're hopeful for. Choosing not to set an intention can, however, limit your creativity and resolve in pregnancy and birth.

When you make a commitment to yourself, your mind begins to imagine possibilities, support, tools, and ways of getting through birth that simply can't be accessed when you shut down emotionally and don't dare to hope. You don't need to share this intention with anyone (especially if you're concerned that people will rain on your parade), although it may be useful to share it with your partner and support team.

What is it that you *really* want for yourself in birth? If you allowed yourself to dream, what would your vision be?

Why is this important to you?

Ask yourself again and again, slowly peeling away societal or family expectations and getting to the root of your desire. Notice how your answer changes the more you write it...

Why is this important to you?

Why is this important to you?

Why is this important to you?

Why is this important to you?

How can you move toward your WHY in a birth that looks different from your intention?

People you will share your intention with:

People you will not share your intention with:

When you have focused your intention for birth, repeat the statement below to help it settle in with just the right amount of gentleness and spaciousness:

> *"I will do my best to move toward this intention. I will not hold it against myself if the birth veers in a different direction, or if I learn something after the birth that may have helped me have a different outcome. I will walk the path of self-compassion as I hold my intention. I will acknowledge the role of grace. I will not expect myself to control an uncontrollable process."*

Plan

Making a birth plan can help you gather information, clarify your intentions, and initiate important conversations with your birth team during pregnancy. When birth plans are not used in awareness, however, they can reduce psychological flexibility and collaborative communication.

Whether you call it a "birth plan" or "birth preferences," this document risks internalizing linear thinking about how birth should go. While it's meaningful to set an intention for what you'd like to happen in your birth, it's also important to prepare for other ways that the birth may unfold. Avoiding hard topics is not a solid plan for avoiding disappointment.

Your Parent archetype knows where you want to go, and also knows that your worth is not dependent on that outcome. As a Parent, you can explore many ways to cope through different scenarios, and how to stay connected to the birth, the baby, your partner, and yourself through an unwished-for outcome.

This gentle and courageous look at unwished-for possibilities gives you more personal power. It gives you the reach to keep going, stay present, and do the next best thing regardless of the outcome.

A positive mindset is not required as part of a holistic approach to birth. You can cry, moan, and groan if things don't go as hoped. You can also get back on your feet and take the next small step forward. Allowing tough emotions to flow through you and doing what the moment calls for are not mutually exclusive.

When you consider your preferences for birth, focus on what *you* will do and how *you* will cope. The birth plan loses its effectiveness when it is focused on trying to control other people.[18] If you feel that you need to try to change other people's behavior, ask yourself if you are in the best birth space, have the ideal care provider for your needs, and have assembled a support team that is likely to show up for you in the way you need them to. Rather than writing down the behavior you want them to change, try having a heart-to-heart conversation or consider making a change to your birth team.

As you look ahead to labor, explore all the possibilities you may need to cope. Instead of telling people not to offer you an epidural for example, tell them how you plan to cope with the pain of labor. After all, the lack of an epidural is the absence of something; it doesn't tell your support team anything about how you plan to work through discomfort and intensity. Circle ideas that you'd like to use below and write down any others you can think of.

---

[18] Pam England, CNM, MA, *Ancient Map for Modern Birth: Preparation, Passage, and Personal Growth during Your Childbearing Year* (Albuquerque: Seven Gates Media, 2017)

Shower
Bath
Foot Soak
Rebozo
Aromatherapy
Cool Compress
Warm Compress
Epidural
Hand Massage
Foot Rub
Back Rub
Chanting
Counterpressure
Pressure Points
Mantra
Prayer
Affirmations
Crying
Slow Dancing
Doula
Vocalizing
Mindfulness Practices

Music
Standing
Leaning
Sitting
Kneeling
Squatting
Lying Down
Birth Ball
Physical Intimacy
Candlelight (Natural or
LED)
Moaning
Singing
Laughing Gas
Focused Breathing
Focal Point
Visualization
Hip Squeeze
Holding Someone's
Hand
Covering the Eyes to
Reduce External

Stimuli
Having Your Hair
Stroked or Played With
Close Eye Contact
Holding a Cherished
Item –
Prayer Beads, the
Baby's Blanket, etc.
Swearing
Turning Inward
Holding Someone Close
Rocking/Swaying
Walking in Nature
Calling a Loved One for
Emotional Support

_____
_____
_____
_____
_____
_____

Rather than thinking of your birth as a linear path, try imagining labor as a tree with many branches. On the unmedicated branch, you have smaller branches attached to it – *mantras, movement, slow dancing, meditation, etc.* The epidural branch connects to the branches of *keeping your partner close by, head massage, switching sides every thirty minutes, visualizing your baby moving through your pelvis, rest, etc.* On the cesarean branch, you have *eye contact with your partner, skin-to-skin in the operating room, gentle music, mindfulness practices, etc.*

Not everything you've imagined to be supportive will happen or feel desirable in labor, but you'll have more creativity and possibilities for how to move through the uncertainty of birth when you stay open to many possibilities for coping.

Opening

Before you begin, you'll need to gather drawing materials. Chalk pastels are ideal, but work with what you have. Even magic markers or a pen will suffice for your process.

When elephants give birth, their herd may gather in a circle around them facing outward. This act of solidarity gives the birthing elephant protection from predators like lions and hyenas in addition to providing privacy for the birth process. When dogs and cats give birth, they will often hide in a dark closet or under a bed or porch, safe from distractions and danger.

Dolphins will have a "midwife" dolphin bring the baby dolphin to the surface for its first breath of air while their parent rests after birth. A seahorse will gyrate his body in the water, moving around to help the baby seahorses emerge. Giraffes give birth by the watering hole where there is easy access to nourishment. Ranchers will sometimes pull calves out with rope to help a birth along. Even animals need technology or medical assistance to birth their babies at times.

Protection, safety, freedom of movement, privacy, food, water, and occasional medical assistance seem to be common needs of birthing mammals, including humans.[19] What else do you suppose you will need to help you open in labor? Write down as many ideas as you can, drawing inspiration from animal and human births. Don't think, don't stop. Go!

Write these words in the frame (outer circle) on the next page. Some important words may repeat. There may even be new words that come to mind as you frame your space for opening in labor.

_____

[19] Based on the "Creating a Birth Space That Will Help Me Open" process from Pam England, CNM, MA, *Our Birthing From Within Keepsake Journal* (Albuquerque: Birthing From Within Books, 2003)

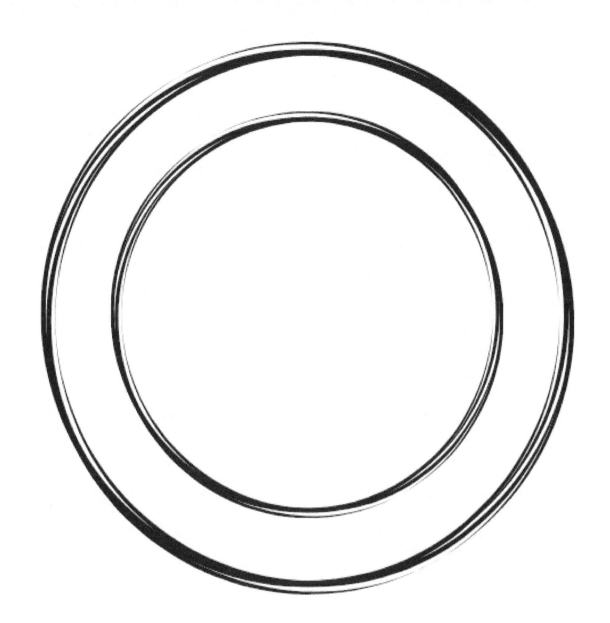

There is great focus on the way the cervix opens in labor, but this pressure on one tiny organ limits awareness of just how much opening takes place when you are transformed by birth.

Beyond the cervix, your pelvis bends and changes shape with help from the hormone Relaxin. It expands to create space for the baby, in cooperation with the muscles, ligaments, and fascia surrounding the pelvis. Your belly opens to intuition, gut knowing, and sensing what to do from one moment to the next – not from your mind, but from the deepest part of your being.

The heart opens to vulnerability, allowing support, love, and connection to flow in from the people around you. It opens to infinite compassion for whoever you need to be and whatever you need to do to bring your baby into the world. Your throat opens to let out prayers, mantras, moans, and primal yells. These sounds emerge spontaneously from the body, shifting with the changing phases of labor and baby's descent through the pelvis. They provide a signal to help wise birth keepers on the outside understand what is happening within you.

Your ears open to let in words of encouragement, the sound of baby's heartbeat, the rush of water in a shower or birth tub, the soothing rhythm of music, and reminders to keep going. Your mind opens to release limiting beliefs, so that old rules about who you have to be can melt away, creating space for your most bare, essential self to emerge.

Draw an image to represent Opening in the center of your frame, using as many symbols, colors, and ideas as you can.[20] When you feel like your drawing is complete, take a moment to listen within. What else is asking to be included in this image of Opening? What else needs to be expressed?

---

[20] Based on the "Creating a Birth Space That Will Help Me Open" process from Pam England, CNM, MA, *Our Birthing From Within Keepsake Journal* (Albuquerque: Birthing From Within Books, 2003)

My Body

In a society where pregnant people are inundated with scary messages about birth, it makes sense that parents want to latch on to faith that birth will work out as they hope. Many pregnant people find solace in the idea that their body was made to give birth.

Although this statement has only positive intentions, it comes with emotional risk. Many parents will be haunted by the silent accompanying belief that if birth doesn't unfold in a particular way, there is something wrong with them or their body. This leaves little room for the unpredictable nature of birth, and ample room for disappointment and feelings of failure if an unwished-for intervention is used during birth.

It is possible to celebrate the wisdom of the body while acknowledging that there are more factors that shape a birth than anatomy. Your body and the baby's body are both incredibly wise. They work in tandem in a dance that is both mysterious and breathtaking. These incredible bodies have more wisdom than our eyes can perceive.

Sometimes a breech baby has a short umbilical cord that prevents it from turning head-down. Sometimes a pregnant body that has become ill births a baby very quickly, seemingly with an inherent knowledge that bringing baby earthside will provide the help they need outside the womb.

If you are going to put your trust in your body's design, then it seems only fair to also trust in your body's intelligence – whether you come to understand it after the birth or not. Do you only trust your body when it's behaving the way you want it to, or can compassion be expanded to include the way your very complex body does the best it can under the circumstances?

The black-and-white thinking that is so common in our birth culture leaves out many birth outcomes and many birthing people. It fails to acknowledge the innumerable factors, seen and unseen, that contribute to the way a birth unfolds.

You can counter the harmful effects of absolute thinking by developing a discerning ear with statements about birth (and parenting). You can examine those words through a compassionate lens to decide whether or not those statements both encourage you and acknowledge your humanity.

How is your body already working well? What is your body doing to help you and your growing baby? Instead of accepting or rejecting your body based on the events of your birth, how can you validate all of the incredible things your uterus, your ovaries, the placenta, the umbilical cord, your skin, your mammary tissue, your pelvis, and all of your other body parts are doing?

Whether your baby is born vaginally or by cesarean, whether your labor begins spontaneously or with an induction, whether you are able to nurse your baby or not, what is a statement of compassion that you could gift to your body and yourself? Write it below.

My body is _____.

You have an opportunity to move away from pressuring, controlling, or blaming your body before the birthing process begins. Instead, notice what's working within your body with a sense of love and gratitude. When your mind shifts from resistance to empathy, you can work *with* whatever situation may arise in labor instead of against it.

Loving Kindness

The loving kindness meditation is a practice that softens the heart and increases empathy.[21] Your connection with yourself is one of the most important relationships to nurture during your preparation for birth. Find a comfortable place to sit where you can rest and be alert at the same time. Bring your focus to each part of your body, beginning with your head and working your way down.

Slowly scan your body, sending loving kindness…

- to your head
- to your mind
- to your eyes and ears
- to your mouth
- your throat
- your chest
- your solar plexus
- your lungs

- your belly
- your womb
- your pelvis
- your vagina
- your thighs
- your calves
- your feet

---

[21] Nancy Bardacke, CNM, *Mindful Birthing: Training the Mind, Body, and Heart for Childbirth and Beyond* (New York, Harper Collins, 2012)

With each breath, allow self-acceptance to envelope you from the crown of your head to the soles of your feet. Feel compassion vibrating through each cell in your body; allow it to seep into the spaces between your cells.

Bring your attention to all of the pieces of your physical and emotional self that you find easy to connect with. Send loving kindness to all the parts of yourself that you like best. Allow yourself to breathe acceptance and gratitude into all of those spaces in your body, with awareness of how easily and naturally this appreciation flows.

Next, notice the parts of your body, your mind, and your personality that you have learned to dislike. Witness the feelings of anger, loneliness, resentment, fear, rejection, or powerlessness associated with them. Those rejected aspects of you are asking for love too.

They are asking to be seen. They want to feel heard. What is the medicine of loving kindness that you can offer these cast-off parts of yourself? Can you acknowledge their pain? Can you begin filling those cracks with the golden epoxy of self-compassion?

How does it feel to offer even a teaspoon of gentleness, forgiveness, and patience to the cast-off parts of yourself? What does the sweet nectar of self-acceptance feel like in your heart and mind?

Repeat this process as often as possible, bringing awareness to the way your relationship with yourself shifts with repetition. Through loving kindness, you will promote a healthy relationship with your body and mind. You will create a layer of protection against self-judgment as you face the challenges of birth and postpartum.

Gate of Doubt

"Stumbling is not falling." — *El-Hajj Malik El-Shabazz (Malcolm X)*

As you move through the labyrinth of birth, you will encounter "gates:" moments when you cross a personal threshold. You'll sense a gate every time you feel stuck, every time there is an opening, and every time you must recommit to the mantra, "Keep going."

Meeting the unexpected for the first time in birth brings you face-to-face with the Gate of Doubt.[22] When you encounter the place where labor diverges from what you had imagined, and you can no longer think your way through the journey, doubt in the process and in yourself can arise.

Rather than resisting doubt or trying to circumvent this gate, allow yourself to become curious about it. "I wonder how long it will take me to reach the Gate of Doubt?" "I wonder what I will need to do, or do differently in order to walk through it?"

---

[22] Pam England, CNM, MA, *Ancient Map for Modern Birth: Preparation, Passage, and Personal Growth during Your Childbearing Year* (Albuquerque: Seven Gates Media, 2017)

Some people say that there's no way to prepare for the unexpected in birth. Others will suggest that you can plan your way out of it. Still others will claim that you can avoid it with positive thinking.

You can prepare to face this gate with courage by bringing awareness to the places where you have encountered the Gate of Doubt in your life already. Become curious about where the Gate of Doubt has surfaced in your work, relationships, and personal life, and how you've managed to move through it.

How do you cope with doubt? What internal resources help you work through it? Which external resources help you get through it? How do you hold on to your compassion and sense of humor when this Gate shows up in your life? Write your observations below.

Opposition

As an expecting parent, you are probably no stranger to the voice of doubt. Co-workers, family members, and even strangers may openly express their doubt in your wishes for the birth. Sometimes that doubt can feel like disdain, or as if the other person feels defensive about their own experience. How do you navigate this sensitive space?

Begin by asking yourself who really needs to know what you're planning for your birth. People who are not emotionally invested in you probably don't deserve the energy it would take to defend your choices, preferences, and ideas. While you don't need to censor yourself, it may feel better to use your energy to prepare your mind and body for birth, rather than convince a person who is peripheral in your life that they're wrong about your wishes.

On the other hand, you may find that some people you share a mutual caring relationship with do not support your choices. This dynamic can be very frustrating and confusing while you walk the line between pursuing your intention and maintaining this important relationship.

When you become curious about the positive intentions behind the words and actions of others, your heart softens, and it becomes easier to connect with them. What do you suppose is this person's positive intention? What is it that they want for you? For your baby? For your relationship? Do they want you to be safe? Do they want to avoid guilt over not bringing up their concerns? What are they really trying to accomplish with their disagreement about your birth choices?

If you want to have a heart-to-heart with this person, begin by meeting them where they are. Acknowledge their positive intention: "I know/I think that you really want _____ for me/the baby/us." You can even thank them for their love and concern. When they feel heard, they may become a little less rigid. They may open up to your perspective and your positive intention because you have been so generous in doing the same for them.

After acknowledging their positive intention, share your positive intention with them. When you talk about intentions, connection, and relationships instead of isolated topics, you nurture interpersonal compassion and connection.

Remember to remain unattached to the outcome of this conversation. You cannot control other people's beliefs or responses, no matter how gentle and compelling your words may be. While they may respond positively, their conditioning and habits may bring out a different reaction – one that you can neither predict nor control. These conversations are still worth having. It's an opportunity for you to practice mindful communication, to assert yourself, and to practice not taking others' responses personally.

Birth Stories

Some people feel compelled to share their birth story in order to avoid feeling guilty about not telling you what could go wrong, or not encouraging you to have the same positive experience that they did. An ancient part of their brain knows that teaching through storytelling is a traditional way to pass on wisdom, but their modern brain may not have learned how to do it in a meaningful way.

The overtones of pride, shame, victimization, and even disdain that shine through these unprocessed stories can feel overwhelming to the listener. Lately, pregnant people have been pushing back on these stories by setting boundaries. Many parents-to-be tell people that they only want to hear positive birth stories.

While this approach is understandable, it's also a missed opportunity. Those who have already been through the ordeal of birth have been initiated into parenthood. Their stories could hold pearls of wisdom for you – not about the specific details of their birth story, but about birth as a rite of passage.

When someone shares their birth story with you, there is an opportunity to shift the conversation and help the encounter become a valuable part of your preparation. Instead of asking questions like which hospital they went to, or how long they pushed for, try asking them questions that speak to the soul of what it means to give birth. For example:[23]

- *When was the first time you felt like a parent?*
- *What was the most meaningful thing someone did for you during the birth?*
- *How did you get through the pain? If you had an epidural, how did you know it was the right time to get an epidural?*
- *What did you learn about yourself from the birth process?*
- *What did you do when you didn't know what to do?*
- *What was one moment when you surprised yourself? When you did something you didn't know you were capable of?*
- *What was most helpful to you in your physical postpartum healing?*
- *What was most helpful to you in your emotional postpartum healing?*

As you shift the conversation about birth to allow friends, family members, and strangers to become birth mentors, write down any nuggets of wisdom below that you would like to remember for your own initiation into parenthood.

---

[23] Introduction to BIRTHING FROM WITHIN Workshop Workbook for Mentors and Doulas ©2000-2010

Gate of Love

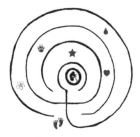

When parents arrive at the Gate of Love[24], the social masks begin to crack and fall off. The usual strategies for gaining love and acceptance take up too much energy at this stage of labor. The roles you play in relationships and society drift further and further from your consciousness. No longer able to uphold old beliefs about how you should move through the world, you drop the cumbersome veil of self-suppression, and allow yourself to do what needs to be done.

At the Gate of Love, you realize that you don't have to look like the people in birth videos, your family members, or your friends in order to be worthy of love and support. In a safe environment, you're able to unguard your heart and create space for an unedited version of yourself to labor.

Sometimes a loss, a transition, the end of a relationship, or a career change requires embodying a more raw and vulnerable part of yourself for a time. Write about a point in your life when the intensity of a situation required you to put down the roles you play in life and accept yourself just as you were in that moment. How did you manage to bring self-love to such a time in your past?

---

[24] Pam England, CNM, MA, *Ancient Map for Modern Birth: Preparation, Passage, and Personal Growth during Your Childbearing Year* (Albuquerque: Seven Gates Media, 2017)

Relationship

Your entire romantic history, including the norms established in your relationship with your current partner, impacts the way you think about relationships. The patterns that you observed between couples and families when you were growing up are also an integral part of your belief system.

These memories, dynamics, and habits affect the way you *engage, disengage, show vulnerability, become guarded, speak your mind, keep the peace, take charge, or follow along*. Throughout your life, you mentally record the "rules of engagement" for how to be in a relationship.

Those rules are intended to protect your basic need for love and acceptance. When you operate under the (learned) belief that these basic needs are conditional and must be earned, your words, actions, and self-expression become limited.

Molding yourself into an uncomfortable shape as a strategy to earn love (whether the other person is aware of this or not), causes you to disconnect from yourself. Which of the italicized traits from above are serving you well? Which ones represent the way you have suppressed a part of yourself to try to earn love?

Birth has a way of pushing people to their limits, taking them to unfamiliar places, and requiring them to act in unfamiliar ways in order to bring their baby into the world. Knowing that this pressure to go beyond the edge of what feels comfortable will almost certainly be part of your birth process, how will it serve you, as well as your partner, to become acquainted with those split-off parts of yourself prenatally?

If you are usually the decision maker in the relationship, experiment with allowing your partner to take the lead. They won't do things "perfectly," or just the way that you would, but perhaps it will allow your partner an opportunity for their own personal growth. This practice of not-doing may also relieve some pressure for you around being in control.

If you typically try to keep the peace instead of speaking your mind, experiment with voicing your opinions more, even in small ways – like telling your partner that you would actually rather *not* go see the action movie they picked out for date night.

Based on your list, what kind of experiment could you create in order to give yourself more personal freedom in your life and your relationship? It doesn't need to be a secret from your partner. They could even help you think of experiments and encourage you to follow through with them.

Keep a log of your relationship experiments below, along with notes about what you learn about yourself, your partner, or your relationship.

Connection

In the whirlwind of day-to-day life, housework, pets, careers, and other responsibilities, it can be hard for expecting parents to find time to connect and focus on birth preparation. That goes double if this is not your first child. Creating a ritual of connection just a couple of times each week can allow you space to focus on your growing family, and help you feel more prepared to navigate the gates of labor as a unified team.

Set an intention together for how much time you will dedicate to this practice of connection and relationship building, and put it in your calendar. You will find two lists below to help make this time together more constructive. The first is a list of ways to physically connect, and the second has discussion prompts to explore together. Choose one item from each category to serve both your physical and emotional preparation for birth.

Physical Touch Cues for Partners

Hand massage: Spread coconut oil or lotion onto the pregnant parent's hand and slowly press from the wrist down each finger, gently squeezing each of their fingers between your thumb and forefinger. Repeat as many times as needed.

Foot rub: Gently rub coconut oil or lotion onto the pregnant parent's foot and lower leg. Hold their foot gently in one hand as you slowly massage their foot with the other hand. Then give slow, firm pressure up the lower leg, helping to increase circulation.

Coupling Touch and Breath: Matching your touch and breath with your partner's breath can help you drop into the same mental space as the pregnant parent. As you rub your hand up and down their back, match your upward movement with their inward breath, and your downward stroke with their outward breath.

Head rub: Slowly run your fingers through your partner's hair, or rub your cupped hand over their hair/head. You can also incorporate gentle scratching with your fingers, like a wire massage comb. They may enjoy having their hair brushed or braided as well.

Cement hands: Plant your hand firmly and lovingly on your partner's lower back, shoulders, belly, or thighs. Allow them to breathe into your grounding touch.

Question Prompts for Parents

Ask one another: What are you most looking forward to about becoming a parent? What are you most nervous about?

Ask one another: What is your favorite memory from when we first met? What's something we do now, or used to do, that you hope to continue doing after the baby is born?

Ask one another: What is a physical attribute or personal trait of mine that you hope the baby gets?

Ask the pregnant parent: What is one thing you would most need from me if the birth doesn't go the way you're hoping? *Be as specific as possible. Responses like, "Support," may be too vague to help well-intentioned partners put your wishes into action.*
Ask the birth partner: What would help you cope if something unexpected happened during the birth? Who could you lean on for support outside of our relationship in that moment?

Ask one another: What do you think we're most likely to argue about after the baby is born? What are some solutions to these conflicts that we can write down now to refer to when we're too tired and stressed to think clearly?[25]

Ask the pregnant parent: What do you think will be most challenging for you to cope with during labor? What is one small thing I could do now, or in the moment, that might relieve some pressure?

---

[25] Pam England, CNM, MA, *Our Birthing From Within Keepsake Journal* (Albuquerque: Birthing From Within Books, 2003)

Ask the birth partner: What do you think will be most challenging for you during the birth? What is one small step we could generate that could help ease up on the intensity of that challenge, if only a little bit, or for only a little while?

Ask the pregnant parent: What is the most vulnerable thing you can imagine doing to get through labor? How can I make it easier for you to be able to do that?
Ask the birth partner: How could you make sure that your own needs are taken care of during the birth (eating, drinking, resting) so that you have enough energy to continue supporting me?

Ask one another: What is something you enjoy doing that you hope to share with the baby? What is something we enjoy doing together that you're looking forward to sharing with the baby?

Ask one another: What is one thing you wish I understood about how the pregnancy and birth preparation is going for you?

Ask one another: If there's one thing that you really wish we could avoid during the postpartum adjustment, what would that be? What is one small thing we could do to cope with that scenario if we can't avoid it?

Ask one another: What might help us work together to work through issues or disagreements about parenting? What might get in the way of us working together? How might we resolve that, or work to remove this obstacle?

Communication

The way you communicate your wishes, needs, and frustrations will likely look different in labor than in your everyday life. The parts of your brain that deal with language and decision-making will power down so that the primitive brain can take over and help your attention turn inward. As you drop into the mental space known as Labor Land, you will lose track of time, and you won't perceive pain with the same intensity that you normally would.

This means that your birth partner can't rely on you speaking your mind as their only means of understanding your needs during labor. The lines of communication may very well go down in order to divert your energy to coping through contractions. Your partner may have to depend more on the support of the birth team, their gut, and your nonverbal cues in order to discern what the moment calls for.

Your birth partner can warm up for Labor Land by practicing reading your nonverbal cues before the birth, noticing what your body language indicates that you want more or less of.[26] That way, they will be well-versed in the language of Labor Land by the time contractions begin.

---

[26] Pam England, CNM, MA and Rob Horowitz, PhD, *Birthing From Within: An Extra-Ordinary Guide to Childbirth Preparation* (Albuquerque: Partera Press, 1998

Discomfort

When you woke up with a sore throat as a child, what was the response from the adults in your household? Were you told to suck it up and get on the school bus? Were you doted on and pampered? Were you given Tylenol and parked in front of the TV?

You can hold the awareness that the people who raised you were doing the best they could, while simultaneously exploring the ways that your early experiences impacted your expectations about how people who are sick or in pain should be treated. By shining a light on these beliefs, it's possible to create more flexibility for yourself in preparation for coping with pain in labor.

Write down the overarching messages you learned about pain and discomfort in your formative years:

Pain is

To cope with pain, I should

When I'm in pain, other people should

Do these messages align with the way you're hoping to approach labor? If not, there may be parts of your ingrained belief system that are asking to be unpacked. What part of your early conditioning about pain is no longer serving you? What would you like to release before you go into labor? Stoicism? Overreliance on or outright rejection of drugs for coping with pain? Narrow views of what acceptable coping looks like? Naming these beliefs is a powerful step toward letting them go. Write the expired beliefs from your medicine cabinet below.

When you become more aware of your past conditioning and identify beliefs and behaviors that no longer serve you, it's possible to look at pain through a wider lens. Complete the journaling excavation below, doing your best to balance your intentions of gentleness and determination.

Pain is

but it could also be

To cope with pain, I would like to

and

and

I can even give myself permission to (swear, cry, be snappy, howl, for example) if it's what I need to get through the birth:

If I were to have _____(unwished-for event)_____ in labor, I could cope by:

I might also cope by: (List as many as you can!)

If I were to have _____(different unwished for event)_____ in labor, I could cope by:

I might also cope by: (List as many as you can!)

When I'm in pain, I hope other people will support me by

and

and

I will discuss this with them on

Voice

While there are many voices in the birth world telling pregnant parents to "speak up" and "advocate for yourself," that notion may directly counter your experiences of interacting with authority figures. Both in school and at home, there's a good chance that you spent time learning to be quiet and compliant in order to gain the approval of the people in charge. With so much practice in being submissive, you may find it challenging to change gears at prenatal check-ups or in the delivery room.

These deep-seated patterns of behavior tend to persist into birth and beyond if left unexamined. The journaling exploration below can help you excavate old beliefs about using your voice, and open up more space to practice this skill.

When I was young, the things I learned about standing up to authority figures were:

I lost my voice when[27]

I learned to behave a certain way in order to gain love and acceptance. Now that I am older, I know that I am inherently worthy, and that love and respect don't have to be earned with self-suppression. With this new awareness, one small thing that I would like to do differently is

Today I feel like I can speak up for myself

1: not at all ⟵⟶ 10: always

If I were to move just one notch up the scale, one thing I would be doing that I hadn't done before is:

_____

[27] Pam England, founder of Birthing From Within and Birth Story Medicine. "Facilitator Training" course, February 2018, Albuquerque, NM

Now run an experiment with this small step, noticing how people receive you, how it feels different in your body, how often it works out, and how often it doesn't go well. If you get discouraged or have less than ideal results, try again. The ability to keep going even when it's tough will serve you well in birth and parenting.

Hypnotized

For modern birthing parents, hypnosis can be used to slow the brain waves, helping parents move from their thinking brain into their instinctual brain and support a more focused mindset. It's important to recognize that hypnosis is not simply a technique to be employed during labor, but a state that we pass in and out of all day long.

In the book *Monsters and Magical Sticks*, Steven Heller, Ph.D. asserts that humans are constantly hypnotized by stimuli in their environment that connects them with old memories, ideas, attitudes, and behaviors.[28]

Have you ever noticed a smell that reminded you of a familiar place from long ago? In an instant, sights, sounds, smells, and words can transport you through time and space, affecting the way you think, feel, and behave. The symbols around you carry powerful hypnotic messages that impact your responses to your environment. You experience this when you find yourself making hot cocoa on a cold day, or feeling a sense of nostalgia when you hear a song from the past.

---

[28] Steven Heller, PhD, *Monsters & Magical Sticks: There's No Such Thing as Hypnosis?* (Original Falcon Press, 2009)

Advertisers know this well, and so do influencers within the medical culture. What is the hypnotic or meta-message associated with putting on a gown with a hospital's name imprinted on it? What meaning do you create about that patient? That medical establishment? That birth?

What do you feel in your body when you name the ideas and beliefs that are related to this image? Is this supportive of helping your body open in birth, or not?

We can rage at the healthcare system, but ultimately most people will birth within it (including some who didn't plan to), which makes this exploration equally important for parents planning to birth outside of the hospital.

The natural birth model carries hypnotic messages as well. What is the meaning that you take from beautiful photos of home births? What does it mean about birth? About birthing parents? What does it mean about who you should be in birth? When you look at photos of parents smiling or looking blissful after birth, who does it tell you that you *should not be* in birth?

By tuning into the over-arching messages behind the symbols that are presented of birth in our culture, you awaken to greater truth and compassion. You can recognize the positive intention of the images and messages you see, without falling under a spell of hypnosis.

How can the symbols of the medical culture and the natural birth culture be re-framed to be more inclusive and supportive of you as a birthing person? If you wind up wearing a hospital gown, is it possible to see it as a ritual garment, like a prayer shawl or a graduation gown, that is only worn in a sacred space or while crossing a personal threshold?

Is it possible to see birth photos as a representation of one of many, many moments within the birth process? Is it possible that you could look very different from that person and still be lovable, worthy, working hard, and doing your best?

How do you create a helpful context for the images and symbols you see in the birth space, and use them to support your journey and expand your self-compassion? Below, write down one element in the birth environment that you feel apprehensive about, whether it be an IV drip, a scalpel, a birth tub, or a fetal monitor. How would you like to reframe this image in order to serve you rather than work against you in birth?

Control

Maintaining control of a situation or yourself allows you to stay in your comfort zone, feeling more at ease and empowered. Staying in control also keeps you out of the arena where transformation and growth take place. The illusion of being able to control the course of your birth ignores the wild, untamed nature of the process. Venturing into the deep water of Labor Land is a requirement of completing the Heroic Journey of birth.

Pushing beyond your comfort zone is the only way to enter the liminal space where the old masks, strategies, and beliefs are cracked open in order for your new self to be birthed. It's the place where you drop from the mind to the heart.

There are many seductive messages in the birth culture about using a birth plan or a positive mindset to assert control over your environment. This message is unfair to the uninitiated parents who are seeking out answers about how to get through birth.

The truth is that birth is hard, that you can count on experiencing uncertainty, and that both of these things are perfectly normal parts of a Rite of Passage. Doubt, struggle, and change during birth do not need to be avoided, controlled, or judged.

If and when you feel a loss of control over your emotions, or environment, or both in labor, what do you want to be reminded of? What is a compassionate statement about who you are in that moment?

Even when I am not in control, I am _____.

Medicine

The most common images of birth that we see in movies and television shows are of people screaming for pain medication. The stories passed down to this generation of expecting parents often contain inductions and epidurals. Giving birth with pain medication has become the cultural default; it is the soup we swim in no matter how you may personally feel about it.

Do the norms of the mainstream birth culture align with your goals, or contrast with the way you're hoping to give birth? What is it that repels you about the parts of birth that you have an aversion to? How do you know to push back against the common culture of birth in this time and place?

Which parts of the modern birth culture are working well for you? A major life change requires a process of evaluation, carefully considering what you will take with you and what you will leave behind.

Think back to all of the messages – explicit and implied – that you have heard or picked up from family, friends, loved ones, media, religion, community, and society. Write them down, including as much variety as you can.

Epidurals are…

Epidurals are…

Epidurals are…

Epidurals are…

Epidurals are…

Epidurals are…

Epidurals are…

Epidurals are…

Epidurals are…

Epidurals are…

Epidurals are…

Remember that all words and actions are motivated by positive intentions and have a basic human need at the root of them. Nestled just beneath the messages you heard about the use of pain medication in labor is the storyteller's need to feel safe, be loved, and belong to a community. Whether or not you agree with others' means of meeting those needs, can you see one or more of them in each of the statements you wrote above?

One person may decide that an epidural will help them avoid doing something embarrassing in labor, satisfying their need to be loved and accepted. Another parent might decide that an epidural could help them avoid trauma after a history of physical abuse, a choice based on their need for safety. Yet another might show disdain toward epidurals (or speak apologetically about having had one) out of an underlying fear of no longer fitting in at their prenatal yoga class or parenting group. This person is motivated by the need to belong to a community. What is your best guess at the need that accompanied each of the statements above that you recorded about epidurals?

What are the basic needs underlying your preferences for birth? Knowing that you never have to share this page with anyone, take a really honest look at the need you're trying to meet in your birth goals for getting through the pain.

Many pregnant parents report wanting to give their baby the best possible start in life, but why? Is it so that you'll feel like a good enough parent? Is it possible that you could be worthy and lovable even if your birth were to unfold in a different way than you're hoping?

Is there anything your baby needs to do to be worthy and lovable? Is there any difference between you and your baby in how much *you* should have to do to earn love and respect? The answer is no.

By taking a far-seeing approach to pain medication, you can see that these decisions do not exist in a vacuum. Rather, they are directly tied to the family, community, and belief systems that you were raised in, and that you currently exist in. They abide within the colliding agendas of the medical birth culture and the natural birth culture. They are connected to long-held beliefs about pain, making noise, asking for help, and being vulnerable. What do you want to remember for birth about this nuanced view of your relationship with pain and pain medication? Journal or draw below.

Time

In a society where efficiency and productivity are held as some of the most valuable qualities, our relationship with the clock can be more contentious than in other cultures. This is reflected on websites that tell you exactly what minute the bus is arriving, the calendar on your smart phone that tells you the exact day and time a task must be done, and apps that time contractions right down to the second. Time is a valuable resource that we ration very carefully. We are aware of our own time, and we're also made aware of the implication of taking up too much of someone else's time.

When you grow up in a "Hurry, hurry, hurry!" environment, that vibration is stored in your mind and body. It seeps into everything you do and the way you respond to the time that your actions and inactions take.

The house I grew up in had a cornfield that neighbored the back of our property. There were some years when the farmers would harvest the corn while people were still wearing shorts and T-shirts, and other years when it wouldn't happen until we had already seen snow.

The farmers knew that the best time to harvest wasn't based on a date on the calendar, but on the condition of the corn. They knew the amount of precipitation that had fallen in the previous year, the amount of dehydration in the corn, and even the way it stood would indicate the best time for harvest, which changed from one year to the next.

Corn grows on horticultural time rather than industrial time, and so do babies[29]. Fifty percent of babies arrive after their due date. Only four percent are born on their actual due date. How does this ambiguity around your due date align with your hopes, ideas, and beliefs about the length of your pregnancy?

What do you consider to be a reasonable length of labor? Do you believe that the progress of your labor should happen at a certain number of centimeters per hour? What do you believe to be true about how quickly changes in your cervix, the baby's position, and your emotional progression through the stages of labor should occur?

---

[29] Nancy Bardacke, CNM, *Mindful Birthing: Training the Mind, Body, and Heart for Childbirth and Beyond* (New York, Harper Collins, 2012)

What would be required of you if your labor were to last longer than you're hoping or anticipating? What might you need to do to sustain yourself through a long labor? What might you need to open up to in order to get through it? With your physical and emotional resources depleted, what will you give yourself permission to do in order to endure a long labor, knowing that it could push you beyond your most familiar and comfortable ways of coping with intensity?

Permission slip: If my labor is very long, I give myself permission to:

If you have a very short labor, how will that align with your ideas about how long labor should take? Sometimes a short labor means that all of the impact from a more average-length labor is packed into a short time, making that birth a very intense ordeal. What beliefs might need to be set aside in order to get through a more fast-moving labor? What is one small thing that might help you let go of ideas about what "should" be, and move through what is, in the best way that you can piece together in the moment?

If you were to visualize your relationship with time as a symbol, what might that symbol be? A giant clock? A starting pistol at the beginning of a race? Something else?

Where in your field of vision do you see this symbol? In front of you, behind you, above you, to the side? How big is it? How much does it weigh? What color is it?

If you were able to change this symbol in some way, what would you want to change about it? The size? The color? Its proximity to you? As your relationship with time becomes more relative, what can you do, or say differently…even this week? What is the first shift that you'll notice when you change your relationship with time?

2nd Trimester Ceremony

By now it's likely that your pregnancy has become obvious, and you are feeling your baby's kicks and wiggles regularly. The transition into the third trimester means that the birth and the baby are becoming more real in your mind. You're seeking out birth classes and perhaps interviewing doulas to begin your birth preparation in earnest.

You may feel like the last few weeks move much faster than the first two trimesters. This sense of flying time can help you feel motivated to dig in and do what needs to be done – physically, logistically, emotionally, and spiritually – to welcome your new baby.

Take time to reflect on the most enjoyable parts of your second trimester, which is often the most pleasant for expecting parents. Did you take a trip with your sweetheart? Did you create a baby registry? Did you get a new wardrobe? Many families wind up moving into a new house or apartment during their pregnancy. Perhaps that life transition is asking to be acknowledged at this time as well.

Gather up symbols around your home or in nature. You can even draw symbols if you like. Choose items that reflect the most enjoyable parts of your pregnancy. Go somewhere in nature where you can find stillness and connection with the earth. This may be your backyard, a local park, a National Forest, a community garden, or a body of water. Express gratitude for the changes that have been happening within your body and your life.

Leave anything there (that will not harm the environment) that you will be working on letting go of in the third trimester.[30] Even if you can't release those things just yet, this ceremony can be a powerful reminder of the work ahead. Now is a good time to consider whether you will need to (and be able to) let go of obligations that weigh on your time and energy – both physical and emotional. This ceremony can acknowledge the parts of your life that are winding down before you start gearing up for the birth.

As you make your way home, keep an eye out for items that symbolize your journey through your final trimester of pregnancy, and the work of preparation and mindfulness that lies before you. Perhaps a rock will remind you of the fierce determination that will be needed to prepare your home, body, and mind for the arrival of your new baby. Perhaps a rose will remind you to soften around expectations of yourself in your final trimester and in labor. Gather as many symbols as you can and keep them in a vase or jar as a reminder of your heart's intention, even when everyday distractions feel like they're pulling your attention elsewhere.

---

[30] Inspired by Francis Weller, *The Wild Edge of Sorrow: Rituals of Renewal and the Sacred Work of Grief* (North Atlantic Books, 2015)

What is your favorite memory of the second trimester?

What surprised you?

What are you most excited about as you step into the third trimester?

What are you feeling apprehensive about as you stand at this threshold?

What resources – internal or external – could help you work through that apprehension? Write as many as you can.

Nest

Oxytocin is the hormone that stimulates contractions, as well as the hormone of love and trust. This hormone thrives in environments where you feel safe, warm, nurtured, and protected.

Endorphins are your body's natural pain killers. They are good friends with oxytocin, and thrive under the same conditions. These hormones flow freely when you feel safe, warm, protected, and have a sense of privacy.

These close-knit hormones both enjoy:

- Slow dancing
- Rhythmic movement
- Repetitive mantra
- Prayer
- Warm, loving touch
- Connection
- Privacy
- Music
- Warm water
- Physical intimacy
- Pleasant aromas
- Dim lighting

Oxytocin and endorphins work in a cyclical rhythm, promoting dilation and progress in the labor, and disrupting pain signals to help the birthing parent cope with the increased intensity.

On the other hand, the flow of oxytocin and endorphins is stifled by the continuous release of stress hormones. Stress hormones are brought on by conditions like:

- Bright lights
- Lack of privacy
- Unwanted guests
- A feeling that you and the staff are working against one another
- Unwanted noise
- Feeling immobilized
- Feeling like you're in a strange or unfamiliar place

Knowing that you can't be nestled in a cocoon throughout the whole labor, you can still welcome as many oxytocin-stimulating elements into your environment as possible, both at home and at your final birth space. These touchstones help support the flow of labor-enhancing and stress-reducing hormones. You can acknowledge that interruptions and distractions are a normal part of life, and then explore how to reintroduce a sense of peace and reinvigorate the flow of helpful hormones to get your mind back on track.

As you begin to assemble your "labor nest" at home, (where you'll likely do your best laboring and work through the majority of your birth) consider what might help you feel safe, loved, and nourished. Lavender essential oil, a warm bath, candlelight, your favorite music, and loving massage are just a few examples of oxytocin-boosters. Write down the comforting items you'd like to have in your nest.

When you move to your hospital or birth center, your new environment can feel surprising to the hormone cycle. Contractions may even slow down for a bit when you first enter this new space. So that contractions are less likely to slow down when you arrive at the hospital or birth center, labor at home for as long as possible. (Talk to your birth team about the best time in labor to arrive.)[31]

Consider what you might bring with you to the hospital or birth center to help it feel a little more like home, especially if it seems at all cold or sterile to you. Would your favorite fuzzy blanket bring you comfort? Your own bathrobe? Christmas lights? Birth art to hang on the walls? A yoga mat in case you feel like kneeling or squatting on the floor? Your own birth ball (also known as a yoga ball or exercise ball) that's inflated just right? What else might help you settle into your new space?

---

[31] Dr. Michel Odent, *Birth Reborn: What Childbirth Should Be* (New York: Random House, Inc., 1984)

If you're planning a home birth, this exploration is important for you, too. When you consider what might help you cope with a change in plans, even in small ways, it gives you more personal power as you get closer to your day of birth. Your mindful consideration of how to navigate a change in location will help you feel more grounded heading into birth, and could decrease the likelihood of trauma if you have to transfer during labor.

Vulnerability

"Vulnerability is the birthplace of innovation, creativity and change." — *Brené Brown*

Vulnerability is a necessary gateway to personal growth and development. In order to be transformed, there must be a falling apart so that you can be put back together in a new way. Much like a snake shedding its skin, you will experience discomfort, friction, and rawness as you give birth to your new self.

Vulnerability sits at the border between the parts of you that you willingly make visible to the world and the parts of you that you keep hidden away. Engaging in vulnerability means opening yourself to potential ridicule, failure, or embarrassment. Sometimes this happens by choice, and other times by force.

It takes incredible courage to choose vulnerability – to let down your guard and allow your whole self to be seen. This courageous act could mean leaving behind the façade that you've got it all figured out. It could mean falling apart or having a huge emotional release. Vulnerability could mean asking for help or saying out loud that you feel lost.

Sometimes when you show vulnerability, you'll be met with disgust or rejection from others. This social exile is always carried out by someone who is disconnected from their own vulnerability, who has carefully constructed a set of strategies to protect their heart from being harmed...again. They criticize you because they are even more critical of themselves, and they deserve compassion for the strategical trap they're caught in.

At other times, however, when you show vulnerability, another person will recognize your deep humanity. They will see themselves reflected in you as you unguard your heart, knowing that the empathy that they give will be reflected back on their own places of vulnerability.

Birth and postpartum take people to deeply vulnerable places by necessity. One cannot be initiated into parenthood in a soulful way without venturing to the depths of their soul. Some people find this place when they are crying out and releasing every bit of force that the intensity of labor propels forth, and some find it when they must agree to doing the very last thing they wanted to do in order to help their baby be born.

There is no one way to pass through the gates of labor, and the way you will navigate through them cannot be planned out ahead of time. You can, however, be inoculated with deep, deep empathy for all parts of yourself. You can also surround yourself with people who are willing to meet you in that place of vulnerability with kindness, patience, understanding, and nurturing.

When in your life have you experienced sincere empathy in a moment of vulnerability? What kind of characteristics did the person have in that moment? Whom could you lean on now, during the birth, and again during postpartum, and feel safe with in your vulnerability?

Open Heart

Before you begin, you'll need to gather drawing materials. Chalk pastels are ideal, but work with what you have. Even magic markers or a pen will suffice for your process.

What would it look like for you to release some, or all, of your strategies of self-protection and unguard your heart? What would have to be given up? What could be gained? In the space below, draw your open heart, allowing images, ideas, questions, and insights to flow through you as the pastel moves across the page. Keep drawing until you feel something shift within.

Affirmation

Many pregnant parents like to create affirmations, either written out on paper or strung up in a style inspired by prayer flags, to keep them encouraged and focused during labor. Rehearsing affirmations helps change the internal dialogue of the unconscious mind. It encourages the brain to move toward solution-focused thinking about your hopes, rather than problem-focused thinking about what you would like to avoid. Affirmations can inspire you to begin acting in a new way, even if you don't fully believe those statements yet.

In order to create affirmations that inspire love and perseverance, rather than judgment or rigid thinking...

- Keep your affirmations focused on you and your baby, not on the people around you.

- Reflect on what you're wanting to move toward, rather than away from. In other words, don't make it a negative. Instead of, "I don't need pain medication to get through this labor," try, "I can cope through hard things."

- Dig deeper. Think about what motivates you to want a certain kind of birth, or to act in a certain way. What is it about a vaginal birth, for example, that appeals to you? Are you wanting to increase the odds of connecting with your baby right after birth?

Focus your affirmation on connecting with your baby, rather than a medical outcome. This creates space for singing to your baby if you can't hold them right away, or connecting by pumping breastmilk if they have to go to the NICU. This makes your affirmation more inclusive and more potent.

Stay away from clichés and overly simplistic messages about birth. "Birth is natural." "Birth is beautiful." "My body opens easily." This limits possibilities rather than expanding them.

Here are a few examples of affirmations that focus on you, are stated positively, dig deeper into heartfelt desires, and aren't attached to a particular birth outcome:

- I am doing my best.
- I send loving kindness to my baby, myself, and my body.
- I am resilient.
- I am opening to what this moment calls for.
- I am loveable, always.
- I am a mother/father/parent.
- I am enough.
- Breath. (The E is left off intentionally. It's a reminder that the breath is there, not a command.)
- Each step forward brings me closer to my baby.
- Birth unfolds on its own time.
- I can focus on what's working in this moment.
- Keep going.

What other affirmations can you think of?

Patience

The discomforts that come with the third trimester can make you understandably sick and tired of being pregnant. Comments from friends, family members, and even strangers predicting an early baby makes giving birth before your due date seem like the normal expectation.

When the people around you express worry about "overdue babies," it reinforces the belief that the due date is a rigid deadline rather than an estimate. When these beliefs are shared casually and frequently, it's easy to become impatient with the pregnancy and birth process.

Pregnancy can be a powerful teacher for you. The lessons won't always be enjoyable, but most lessons worth learning come through struggle, discomfort, and sometimes pain. By learning to be patient with the process and yourself, you will be nurturing an important skill for parenting. Yes, it will be helpful for your child, but it will also help *you* feel less stress and anxiety when you develop patience for what it takes to give birth and parent.

In order to cultivate patience, you might develop a meditation practice, tend to a garden, or participate in a slow yoga class. Attune to the seasons and the gradual changes that come with them. Walk a labyrinth, make a quilt for the baby, or practice the art of "not-doing."

How else could you foster patience as you get closer to birth, and to becoming a parent?

Community

In the colonial United States, the community would attend to parents during birth, and then take turns caring for and feeding the family during the first forty days postpartum. At the end of the initial postpartum period, a "groaning party" would be held to celebrate and thank those who came together on behalf of the growing family. No one was paid for this work. It was simply understood that people would participate in this ritual, and then benefit from it when it was their time to have a baby.[32]

In the nineteenth and early-twentieth centuries, African American "granny midwives" in the southern United States would walk for miles to care for birthing families of all races, often for little or no pay. They would stay with the family for days afterwards, making sure that the parent and baby were healthy, and teaching the family how to feed and care for the baby.[33]

---

[32] Richard W. Wertz and Dorothy C. Wertz, *Lying-In: A History of Childbirth in America* (US: The Free Press, 1977)

[33] Onnie Lee Logan, *Motherwit: An Alabama Midwife's Story* (San Francisco: Untreed Reads Publishing, LLC, 2014)

Parents in Northern India traditionally live with their own parents for a time after the birth so that they receive the rest and care they need. Healing foods are prepared for the recovering parent, and their elders massage them with stress-reducing balms like sesame oil.[34]

All around the world, we see examples of community taking care of growing families, providing education, compassion, wisdom, and support as they navigate the birth process and adjust to life with a new baby. Being held by a community improves mental health outcomes for parents, easing the challenges of crossing the threshold into their new role in life.[35]

These traditional practices stand in stark contrast to the way birth and postpartum are treated in the United States today. Due to failures in public policy about growing families, many parents must return to work and enroll their baby in daycare sooner than puppies are legally allowed to be separated from their mothers. It is not uncommon for parents to return to work before their postpartum bleeding has even finished.

---

[34]Being the Parent Staff Writer, "Traditional Indian Postpartum Care" (blog), Being the Parent.com. https://www.beingtheparent.com/traditional-indian-postpartum-care/

[35] Kimberly Ann Johnson, *The Fourth Trimester: A Postpartum Guide to Healing Your Body, Balancing Your Emotions, and Restoring Your Vitality* (Boulder: Shambhala Productions, Inc., 2017)

Melissa delivered her second child, a beautiful baby girl by repeat cesarean. Living paycheck-to-paycheck, she had no choice but to return to work waiting tables two weeks after giving birth. Her body ached, she was exhausted, and she missed her baby and toddler. Only later did she realize that under all of that pressure and pain, she was suffering from postpartum depression. Looking back on her experience, Melissa said, "I had enough people telling me how hard it was all going to be, but not enough people to believe in me and guide me."

Partners often have even less time for family leave after the birth of a new baby. Even if one parent is able to/wants to stay home and care for the baby, they usually do so in isolation, spending the entire day caring for their child(ren) on their own. This system has put very stressful demands on growing families, making it a struggle for parents to meet both their children's needs and their own.

What's missing is a network of loved ones to care for growing families. While this used to be built into society, it must now be consciously and intentionally constructed by many family units. This is no easy task for parents who may live far away from their extended family, have few community ties, or struggle with asking for help.

Although it doesn't feel like there's extra time and energy to go around during pregnancy, this is an ideal time to work on constructing a community of support to help carry you through the postpartum period and beyond. This is much harder to accomplish when you're operating on limited sleep, recovering from birth, and trying to meet the needs of a brand-new baby.

You can begin seeking out peers, mentors, and elders to fill in any gaps in your support system prenatally. You might find these people....

- In a postpartum support group. (Yes, you can attend while you're pregnant!) La Leche League, babywearing groups, and gatherings for parents are a great place to find camaraderie and support.
- In a faith community, at work, or in other social circles.
- In your neighborhood. There may be other parents, or even elders in your neighborhood who could lend a hand or bring a meal after the baby is born.
- In a childbirth class. Some parents make lifelong friends in birth classes, where they can find peers whose families will share similar milestones.
- From parents, grandparents, or the parents and grandparents of friends.

Remember, not everyone will be well-suited to all types of support. Some will be better at folding laundry, others will cook delicious food, and still others will help you laugh through the hard times. Some helpers will be by your side for a lifetime, and others just for a season. Each has their own important role to play in your network of postpartum and parenting support.

Who are the people in your life who could be part of your postpartum community? Write their names below, as well as how you imagine they could support you during your transition to life with a newborn. Remember, when you open yourself up to asking for help, you allow people to feel a deeper connection with you. You give your friends, acquaintances, and family members an opportunity to feel like they serve an important purpose in your life. You participate in a circle of people who can take turns showing up for one another and leaning on each other for support.

Ancestors

In Nigerian families, it is traditional for the grandmother to give a baby its first bath. This ceremonial act shows the baby's parents that they are not alone in caring for their child.[36]

Connecting with your roots is an opportunity to find solace in the place of belonging – to a family, a community, and an identity. Grounding yourself in culture can help you feel less alone during this major life transition, linking you to those who came before you, and all who will come after you.

Your ancestors serve as a powerful confirmation that many, many people before you managed to give birth – in caves, in bedrooms, under the stars, in operating rooms, on boats. They gave birth alone or surrounded by others. Your ancestors can remind you that feeling excitement, doubt, overwhelm, joy, anticipation, and uncertainty are part of your lineage. How powerful it is to imagine the ways that your family members before you faced these emotional gates leading to parenthood and somehow found the courage to step through them, into the unknown.

---

[36] Ilze Ievina "Newborn Rituals around the World" (blog) Let the Journey Begin. (August, 2016) **https://www.letthejourneybegin.eu/newborn-rituals-around-the-world/**

As people have moved around the globe, many have lost parts of their culture – perhaps because blending in helped them survive in a new country, perhaps because their ancestors were stolen or evicted from their native land and separated from everything they ever knew, or perhaps they lost touch with their roots for another reason.

If you feel disconnected from your culture, ask family and community members what they know about your ancestors and their customs around birth and postpartum. Connect with cultural experts from your family's native soil. Breathe in the values that have been passed down as part of your lineage. Imagine how those who came before you would have treated the childbearing year.

Below, record any stories or traditions from your family pertaining to pregnancy, birth, and postpartum. Which ones warm your heart? Which ones catch your attention? Are there any you would like to take up for yourself? Set aside? Does your partner's family have any special traditions related to the childbearing year that you would like to incorporate into your preparation, your coping, or your healing?

Heirloom

You have been continuously learning about parenting since you were a newborn yourself. You first learned from your own parents, grandparents, and family members what it means to care for a child. You internalized lessons about how much time parents should spend with their kids, what kind of activities they should do together, how they should connect, and how they should set boundaries.

Later, you became acquainted with friends' parents and your kaleidoscope of beliefs about parenting likely twisted, expanding or shifting your image of what it means to be a parent. As you have experienced more of the world and the diverse people in it, your kaleidoscope has probably shifted multiple times over the years. Some elements have changed and others remained the same.

Inevitably, some of the lessons you learned from your parents will be recorded in your book of "Things I'll Never Do When I Have Kids." Other lessons are like heirlooms that you'd like to pass down from one generation to the next. These may be traditions, sayings, ways of being, or attributes that you would like to gift to your child. My father gave me the gift of drumming, and it's something that I hand down to my children. My mother gave me the value of being true to your word, and it's something I try to impart to my little ones.

When you look back on what you've learned from your parents, what is the heirloom that you would like to pass on to your baby? What attribute or tradition from your parents would you like to share with your own child?

Parent

Before you begin, you'll need to gather drawing materials. Chalk pastels are ideal, but work with what you have. Even magic markers or a pen will suffice for your process.

As you scan through your life, reflect on profound parenting moments that you can remember being part of or witnessing. You might have memories of being pushed on the swing by one of your parents, of being scolded, or being guided. You have also seen other parents interacting with their child in ways that warmed your heart or alarmed you.

On the next page, record symbols and images of distinctive parenting moments that captured your attention. You can even capture images of your hopes for how you will parent, or what you're still unsure about when you think of raising a child. Draw as many symbols and images as you can think of, even if they don't make sense or seem to fit together.

When your drawing is complete, take time to journal about your art process. How did it impact the way you view parenting, and yourself, to put all of these images together on the same paper? What did you learn about yourself and about parenting from this exploration?

Enough

As your belly grows and you begin to collect clothing, toys, and diapers for your baby, your mind will naturally dream of the future – imagining what life with your new child will be like and what kind of parent you hope to be. You create plans about what kinds of food you will feed your baby, how you will discipline your child, how you will connect with them, and how you will teach them. How do you envision the Ideal Parent? What do they do?

In your reveries, you probably also imagine what kind of parent you hope *not* to be – your vision of the Substandard Parent. From other people's examples, or even the example of your own parents, you have clear ideas about how you don't want to treat your child, the kinds of influences you want to keep out of their life, and the types of parenting choices that seem negative and unhelpful. What are you hoping to avoid as a parent?

Between the Idealized Parent and the Substandard Parent lies another way of raising children: The Good Enough Parent[37]. What do you suppose a good enough parent would do? What would they say? How would you know if you spotted one? Write down your ideas of what a Good Enough Parent would be or do:

While we all want to provide a great childhood for our little ones, it's simply not possible to be an outstanding parent all the time. You are a human with needs and limitations. You will inevitably be tired, or sick, or grouchy, or forgetful, or fed up at times. Rather than judge yourself against an unattainable standard, you have an opportunity before your child is born to cultivate self-compassion as a parent. You will be better prepared to weather the highs and lows of parenting when you set realistic and kind expectations of yourself.

In his bestseller *The Four Agreements*, Toltec master don Miguel Ruiz explains, "Your best is going to change from moment to moment; it will be different when you are healthy as opposed to sick. Under any circumstance, simply do your best, and you will avoid self-judgment, self-abuse and regret."[38]

Do your best for yourself and your child. Your best will be good enough.

---

[37] Pam England, CNM, MA, *Ancient Map for Modern Birth: Preparation, Passage, and Personal Growth during Your Childbearing Year* (Albuquerque: Seven Gates Media, 2017)

[38] don Miguel Ruiz, MD and Janet Mills, *The Four Agreements: A Practical Guide to Personal Freedom (A Toltec Wisdom Book)* (San Rafael: Amber-Allen Publishing, Inc., 1997)

Gate of Great Determination

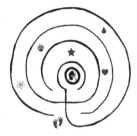

At the Gate of Great Determination[39], you will encounter an unexpected challenge that requires you to dig deep to find strength, courage, or permission to do whatever it takes to birth your baby. This Gate is defined by a moment of surrender to the birth process.

To surrender is not a simple choice to be made, like picking an item off a menu. Surrender only happens in a significant way when you are pushed to the very edge of everything you know. It happens when you have no idea what to do next, and you must rely on something outside of your knowledge base or comfort zone. At this gate, you take a leap of faith because it's the only thing left to do.

---

[39] Pam England, CNM, MA, *Ancient Map for Modern Birth: Preparation, Passage, and Personal Growth during Your Childbearing Year* (Albuquerque: Seven Gates Media, 2017)

When in your life have you had to surrender to the circumstances and find another way through? How did you manage to surrender? What did you learn about yourself through that process?

Fear

Our birth culture is rife with fear-based messaging about pregnant people, pregnant bodies, birth, and postpartum that can easily leave expecting parents feeling frozen and overwhelmed. Some people try to offset these messages by avoiding fear altogether. They may ceremonially burn their fears without acknowledging the roots they sprouted from. Others try to obliterate fear by gathering facts and data about birth. These strategies for avoidance don't help parents cultivate the resources needed to face their fears with courage and resolve.

There is a popular belief that thinking about your fears will cause them to happen. Studies have shown that refusing to think about the unwished-for limits a person's ability to explore how they could cope with a challenging outcome, and is more likely to leave them shocked and traumatized if this undesired event should happen.[40]

---

[40] Barbara Ehrenreich, *Bright-Sided: How the Relentless Promotion of Positive Thinking Has Undermined America* (New York, Metropolitan Books, 2009)

When someone is stuck in resistance, it can become hard for their labor to progress. The cervix, the canal between the uterus and vagina, is a shy organ that opens most willingly when a person feels secure.[41] Even during pregnancy, stressing about the future can make the pelvis and psoas muscle (a long muscle that connects the upper and lower body through the pelvis) tight[42]. Acknowledging worries and exploring solutions can help parents' bodies work more synchronously with them both in pregnancy and in labor.

By becoming curious and solution-focused about worries, you can mobilize your creative resources to imagine yourself moving through the unwished-for with your self-compassion intact. You can see yourself taking action on behalf of yourself, without attachment to that action changing the overall outcome.

Fear, concern, and worry are all normal parts of pregnancy. It's a customary part of the preparation for any journey of significance. Even if they seem silly or trivial, jot down the worries that visit your mental space most frequently. Try to find the snapshot images that you see, or want to avoid seeing, in your mind when you think of these topics.

Choose one of your worries to take a closer look at. What do you see, hear, and feel in this image? What is happening around you? What are people doing, saying, or perhaps not doing? What are you telling yourself it means about you?

---

[41] Ina May Gaskin, *Ina May's Guide to Childbirth* (New York: Bantam Dell, 2003)

[42] Why is the psoas such a major player in our physical, mental and emotional wellbeing?" (blog) EckhartYoga (2018) **https://www.ekhartyoga.com/articles/anatomy/stretching-your-stress-out-meet-your-psoas**

In this snapshot, I am _____.

You will likely feel a visceral response in your body – a sinking in your stomach, a closing in your throat, a tightness in your chest – when you find the negative belief that you carry as the caption for this unwanted event.

> *When you watch a nature documentary, you can see prey animals being chased by predators. Just before they are attacked, their bodies freeze. This response is a self-protection mechanism that helps the prey animal not experience extreme pain and suffering during the attack.*
>
> *However, if the lion stumbles and the gazelle has a window of opportunity, they regain their ability to flee. They will often shake after this encounter, to help work out the adrenaline that was flowing through their body during the attack. Taking action and shaking off the scary event helps animals avoid suffering from symptoms of trauma after the ambush is over.*[43]

What are the implications of this built-in system for human mammals in birth? For one, it means that it is perfectly normal to have a momentary freeze – a jolt of shock or surprise when something alarming happens. It also means that if you can take action – even something as simple as reaching out for a hand to hold – you are less likely to suffer trauma. The action taken doesn't have to change the outcome in order to help you avoid ongoing emotional distress.

---

[43] Peter A. Levine, *Waking the Tiger: Healing Trauma* (North Atlantic Books, 1997)

Taking another look at your snapshot unwished-for image, how do you see yourself taking one small action in this scenario, showing up for yourself in an intense moment even when it doesn't change the outcome?

What attribute would you need from yourself in order to take this action? Self-love? Kindness? Determination? Something else?

Holding that attribute in your mind and your heart, take another look at your snapshot image. What do you know to be more accurate about yourself than your negative belief? What does the wise, empathetic part of yourself know to be true about you in this snapshot?

Even though this has happened, I am _____.

Breathe that new, truer belief into every cell in your body, knowing that this is the real truth about you. Breathe it into your heart where it will stay with you like a drumbeat through the birth and beyond. Breathe it in until you can feel it vibrating through every cell in your being.

Compassionate Cesarean

In many developed nations, parents and birth professionals are fighting to lower the cesarean birth rate. The role of birth activists is incredibly valuable, and also cannot be worked out in the same space as parents whose rite of passage is taking place in an operating room.

There is no doubt that the cesarean birth rate is much too high in many countries around the world. There is also no doubt that parents will continue to give birth by cesarean, due to impatience, fear, or medical necessity. Under the influence of hormones, fatigue, confusion, and concern for the baby, the exact reasoning or degree of necessity for a cesarean birth won't always be clear.

This leaves parents in a tough spot as they prepare to give birth. It is possible to be frustrated by the system that has created a cesarean epidemic, and to also prepare to birth by cesarean in awareness. It is useful for all parents to consider how they could cope through a cesarean birth, and how they could stay connected to their baby, their partner, the birth team, the birth process, and themselves if their baby is born via cesarean.

The first step in fostering a mindful approach to cesarean birth is to bring awareness to the language you use. What kind of imagery comes to mind when you hear that someone "had to have a c-section?"[44] Draw or write your thoughts below.

Now, how does that imagery change when you hear that someone "gave birth by cesarean?" Draw or write your thoughts below.

While a birthing parent should no longer feel physical pain by the time they're settled into the operating room, they can still draw on the coping skills they learned prenatally to help them manage any mental chatter over unexpected or undesired circumstances. The same skills that facilitate your ability to work through contractions can help take the edge off your fear or anxiety while you're getting ready to meet your baby.

---

[44] Pam England, CNM, MA and Rob Horowitz, PhD, *Birthing From Within: An Extra-Ordinary Guide to Childbirth Preparation* (Albuquerque: Partera Press, 1998)

Did you learn breathing exercises prenatally? Did you create a playlist for birth? Were there encouraging words you planned to have your partner say to you when the going gets tough? Now is the time to draw on all of those resources. What else do you suppose you could do to cope with the stress of being in the operating room before your partner is able to join you? How else could you cope while they are by your side? Write as many ideas as you can.

Keep in mind that partners can touch the birthing parent's head, face, and arms – anything outside of the sterile field beyond the drape, which is hung at chest level. They can make close eye contact with their loved one, kiss their forehead, and say kind words.

What do you suppose your partner could do to help you stay present in a cesarean birth, and help you feel seen and supported? Write as much as you can. Ask friends who have given birth by cesarean what helped them cope.

How could you stay connected to your baby during a cesarean birth? Would you sing aloud to them? Would you imagine what it will be like to meet them for the first time? Would you pray for them? In some hospitals, they even lower the sterile drape or use a clear drape so that the birthing parent can see their baby come into the world. Some hospitals will also support parents with immediate skin-to-skin in the operating room after a cesarean birth. List as many ways as you can think of to connect with your baby. Make a star next to any items that you need to speak with your birth attendant about prenatally.

Alisa Voss Godfrey is a midwife in San Antonio whose client had to transfer from a home birth to the hospital where she would give birth by cesarean. The mother was so drowsy from the medicine she had been given that she looked like she was asleep on the operating table. Alisa spoke over her client, telling her that it was time to push her baby out, that she was going to "push from her heart," not knowing whether or not the mother could hear her.

The next day, the mother told her midwife that she had heard everything, and expressed her gratitude for Alisa's loving guidance in taking one small step to stay connected to her baby and the birth process.

If you are reading this after giving birth, you can create a ceremonial time and space to push from your heart, whether or not your baby is present for this ceremony. You can consciously connect with the love and sacrifice that it took to birth your baby by cesarean, and give one last energetic push with your hand on your heart. Push out any doubt and self-judgment that are no longer serving you. Invite in love, compassion, and acknowledgement of your journey.

No matter how a baby is born, all parents need space to grieve pieces of their birth that were disappointing. Not everyone knows how to hold space for another person's disappointment, but perhaps you know one or two people who are empathetic listeners. If so, write their names below to remind you of allies to contact if you need a compassionate ear.

You can also find time to make art or journal to work through any lingering negative feelings about the birth. A trained Birth Story Mentor[45] can support you in changing your relationship with an upsetting birth story. You can also see a counselor to help you work through your difficult feelings about the birth. Write down the internal and external resources below that might be helpful if you find yourself feeling disappointed about your birth experience.

---

[45] **http://www.BirthStoryMedicine.com**

Finally, imagine what your baby would say about you if they could talk. How would your baby describe your love and sacrifice? What would they want to thank you for? Write about your efforts from the baby's perspective below.

It can be difficult to look closely at cesarean birth. Give yourself time to think and process if you need to. Make a commitment to revisit this chapter in a week and see if any new ideas or inspiration come to you for how you could cope and stay connected during a cesarean birth. Imagine it as an emotional safety net that you are weaving over time.

Gate of Holy Terror

"The cave you are afraid to enter holds the treasure that you seek." – Joseph Campbell

One of the signposts that you're nearing the end of labor is feeling exasperated, untethered, and like you don't want to do it anymore. When intensity and hormones combine in transition to bring anxiety, overwhelm, and sometimes even the feeling that you won't make it through, it means that you're getting close to meeting your baby. At the Gate of Holy Terror[46], you must do something you thought you could never do.

---

[46] Pam England, CNM, MA, *Ancient Map for Modern Birth: Preparation, Passage, and Personal Growth during Your Childbearing Year* (Albuquerque: Seven Gates Media, 2017)

In the Heroic Journey, this threshold is called the One Forbidden Thing[47] – a moment when the initiate must do something that all of their conditioning has led them to believe that they should not do. They may need to whine, cry, say they're giving up, snap at a partner or support person, or make a lot of noise. Each person's One Forbidden Thing is unique to their beliefs and upbringing. The One Forbidden Thing can be a gateway to expanded personal freedom, or the catalyst for shame and self-judgment.

When you think about having to do something you really don't want to do to get through labor, what do you imagine? What is the one thing that you really hope you won't have to do?

When you delve into the most creative parts of your mind, what do you know about how it could serve you to do this One Forbidden Thing at the Gate of Holy Terror? Could screaming bring a release? Could snapping at people be the most resourceful way you can communicate your needs under the circumstances? Could saying, "I can't do it anymore!" be a way of letting people know that you need more help? Journal about the potential value of your One Forbidden Thing below.

---

[47] Episode 2 – "The Message of the Myth," Joseph Campbell and the Power of Myth (May 30, 1988) Public Affairs Television and Alvin H. Permutter, Inc. ©

When your most compassionate self rises above this scene, taking an eagle's eye view of the intensity of labor and all of the physical and emotional energy it takes to get through it, what shifts in the way you see the One Forbidden Thing? Fostering gentleness for this part of yourself before the birth just might be the key to passing through the Gate of Holy Terror. Write as much as you can as fast as you can.

Birth Song

Your relationship with sound in labor intersects with old stories about bringing attention to yourself. It's impacted by beliefs about complaining, making a fuss, or being whiny. Early conditioning creates a constellation of rules that can bring a damper to your voice and self-expression in labor, and can cause you to deny yourself of a very natural and effective laboring tool.

If you've ever picked up a heavy box or stubbed your toe on a door, you've probably experienced the relief that came from vocalization. Those expressions of sound often come along with contractions in labor, and can help to dissipate the pain. When you have some space and privacy, alone or with your partner, try making sounds that come from different parts of your body.

What happens when you bring an "Ahhhhhhhhh" sound up from your throat? What happens when you bring that sound up from your chest, your belly, or even your cervix? Notice how the pitch becomes lower, or the way your shoulders move down away from your ears. There is no wrong sound to make in labor. Some can be more helpful than others in releasing tension and helping you move the pain out of your body. Experiment to see what works best for you. You can even try it while holding ice or immersing your hand in ice water.

If you feel shy about being witnessed in a state other than your everyday social self, then you may be someone who needs a more private birth setting and a smaller birth team. If you feel most comfortable when you have multiple people focusing on you and supporting you through challenges, then using your voice may not be as much of a struggle.

You cannot count on being loud or quiet during birth because that's the way you normally behave. In labor, you meet a different side of yourself, including parts that you don't usually share with the world. How might it serve you to surround yourself with people who could support you in your most vulnerable state, or defend your right to do so?

What do you believe to be true about complaining? Has speaking your mind been encouraged or shunned throughout your life? What gained you love and approval as you were learning to make your way through the world and be a good person? Were you taught to let it out, or to stuff your emotions down?

What does the part of you that has been silenced need to hear from your higher self in order to allow you to moan, groan, whine, chant, sing, howl, or bleat your way through labor? Write a letter to yourself on the next page, telling those forgotten and abandoned parts of yourself what they really need to hear about self-expression.

A letter to myself:

Finding the Center

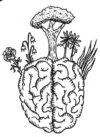

As contractions near peak intensity in labor, you may find a threshold where it takes more effort to push your mind away from the pain than it does to allow your focus to go squarely to the center of it. [48]

The physical sensation of pain is not constant. If you've ever hit your head, you may have noticed that there was a difference between the initial shock, the wave of hurt that followed, and the way the feeling changed once your brain received the signal to release endorphins. Over the coming days or weeks as it healed, your pain may have moved from a sharp stabbing, to an ache, to a sting, to an itch.

When you bring your full attention and curiosity to the sensation of pain, you will notice that it constantly shifts and evolves. As you hold ice cubes, notice where the very center of that sensation lands in your hand. Much like an optical illusion puzzle, a balance of focus and openness will reveal that the location of the most painful sensation migrates from one place to another. It may move closer to your thumb or closer to your wrist without the ice moving at all. Track it like a hunting tiger to see how it expands, contracts, and changes from one moment to the next.

---

[48] Pam England, CNM, MA and Rob Horowitz, PhD, *Birthing From Within: An Extra-Ordinary Guide to Childbirth Preparation* (Albuquerque: Partera Press, 1998)

As you focus the lens of your mental microscope even more, notice that the feeling of the ice changes throughout the 1-minute "ice contraction" as well. It may begin with jabbing pain, drift into a burning sensation, then an ache, and return again to sharpness. While your mind is busy watching the images change on the flickering screen of pain and intensity, it finds itself too busy focusing on these changes to devote its energy to creating a suffering story. [49]

Taking your practice deeper and deeper with each new ice contraction, allow yourself to notice the imagery you associate with the ever-changing sensations of the ice in your hand. You may see fire when the ice burns or sinking wet sand as the ache sinks into your skin. In the next moment, you may find yourself remembering a time when you stood outside catching snowflakes on your tongue on a cold winter night. Continue to track these images, sensations, and movements without attachment or avoidance. Don't try to control or change them. Don't think. Don't stop.

---

[49] Pam England, CNM, MA and Rob Horowitz, PhD, *Birthing From Within: An Extra-Ordinary Guide to Childbirth Preparation* (Albuquerque: Partera Press, 1998)

Intuition

"If you do not listen to your intuition, it will stop talking to you. Your intuition is like a sensitive friend. If you question it, censor it, judge it, it gets hurt and becomes silent."–
Michele Cassou

Fear and intuition abide in such close proximity that it's often hard to differentiate between the two. They both cause a strong visceral response in your body, making it difficult to discern whether the feeling you're getting comes from a place of intuition or fear.

Knowing this can help you to be gentle with yourself during labor, where this fine line becomes even more elusive as stress, fatigue, and hormones make it more challenging to process what's happening. The questions below can help you unravel this mystery if you find yourself having to make a decision under pressure…

1) What do you notice in your body? Do you feel a grounded knowing in your gut, or an anxious sensation of avoidance, like tightness in your throat? Just bringing your awareness to the way this sensation manifests in your body could be a helpful clue in determining whether you're working from intuition or fear.

2) Are you trying to achieve a specific outcome? Aside from keeping you and your baby safe, is there a secondary outcome that you're seeking? Ask yourself, "How do I know to do what I'm doing?" You could utilize the practice of asking yourself *why* five times, moving deeper and deeper into your motivation with each repetition.

If this inquiry shows you that you're worried about taking up too much of people's time, or that you really don't want the midwife to be annoyed with you, then you are acting on fear. This is the time to send yourself an infusion of love and acceptance (you can ask the people around you to help you with this task as well), and see if your intuition gives you a sign beyond the fear-based strategies for avoiding discomfort.

3) Do you feel rushed? You are more likely to make decisions from fear when you feel pressured to give an answer quickly. Asking for a few minutes to think can give your nervous system a chance to settle and make it easier for you to access intuitive knowing.

> *Janet had ascertained from birth images and medical models that lying down in labor would be counterintuitive and unhelpful, but she found herself utterly exhausted as the intensity of contractions increased. Near the end of labor, she crossed a threshold of releasing the beliefs and expectations she had learned and lay down to rest. She felt relief as she responded to what the labor, her intuition, and her body were asking of her.*

Think of a time when you were able to connect with your intuition. What did you notice in your body, your mind, or your environment that made this possible?

Now think of an instance when you made a decision based in fear. What was happening in your mind, body, and environment at that time?

What were the subtle (or not so subtle) differences between these two experiences? How could this help you differentiate between fear and intuition during your pregnancy, birth, and postpartum?

Forgiveness

Long before you ever have your first contraction, you can probably identify what you hope you won't have to do in labor. "I hope I don't lose control." "I hope I don't cry." "I hope I don't make too much noise." "I hope I won't be mean to my partner."

It's hard to imagine behaving in a way that's completely out of the ordinary for you. Perhaps you don't want to upset the other people in the room, cause an unpleasant experience for someone else, or have your partner or birth attendants be upset with you.

Bear in mind that doctors, midwives, nurses, and doulas have a very wide spectrum of what they see as "normal" behavior in labor. It's probable that whatever you do to get through contractions won't be new for them, even though it may be very new for you.

Most birth partners go into childbirth with an acceptance of whatever their pregnant loved one needs to do to get the baby out. This means that there is likely only one person you would have to ask forgiveness from regarding what happens during labor – *yourself.*

When you start taking away ingredients for coping because they would be too embarrassing, rude, or wild, you have less material to work with. The more you can leave in your coping pantry, the more creative and flexible you can be during labor. Since birth is unpredictable, it's good to keep the chili powder in your kitchen just as accessible as the sugar.

The good news about self-forgiveness is that you can do it before giving birth. Write below one item (or more if you like) that might be really useful to offer yourself forgiveness for before your labor begins.

How would you like to release the guilt or shame attached to this ingredient that you've now committed to allowing in your pantry, even if you don't wind up using it? The elements of nature have an amazing power to transform[50]. Your shame and guilt can be written on (biodegradable) paper, leaves, or sticks and handed over to a river to carry away, buried for the Earth to transform, or burned and turned into smoke, like a prayer for self-compassion floating into the air. How will you create ceremonial transformation of the walls that have been put up in your heart to block out doing whatever it takes to birth your baby?

_____

[50] Francis Weller, *The Wild Edge of Sorrow: Rituals of Renewal and the Sacred Work of Grief* (North Atlantic Books, 2015)

Intensity

Before you begin, you'll need to gather drawing materials. Chalk pastels are ideal, but work with what you have. Even magic markers or a pen will suffice for your process.

Imagine a really tough contraction – one that lasts over a minute and is accompanied by nausea, overwhelm, and looking for a way out. How severe do you imagine that intensity to be? If you had to give it a number, a name, or a color, what would represent the most intense part of labor, based on everything you know right now? Write or draw it in the center circle on the next page.

On the outside circle, write as many ways as you can think of to help you cope with this level of intensity. Changing positions, connecting with a birth companion, or breathing in a certain way are some of the most common ideas I've heard pregnant parents mention. While these methods wouldn't take away the pain, they could change the amount of suffering you experience.

Write as many coping ideas as you can around the outside circle – even the ones that seem silly, impractical, or dramatic. Continue to ask, "What else? What else? What else?" as you explore your internal resources.

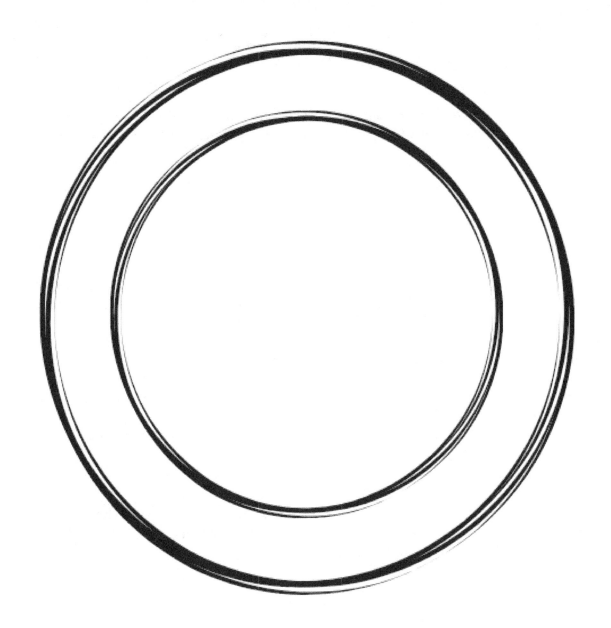

Now, just for a moment, imagine if that pain were just a little stronger than you imagined. How might that number, word, or symbol change? Add anything you need to the center circle to represent this increase.

As you drop in and connect with the most resilient, creative, and flexible parts of yourself, begin to explore *what else* you might need to do to get through the intensity of labor at this higher altitude.[51] What might be asked of you that wasn't required with your previous symbol? How many ways of coping could you give yourself permission to bring into your birth in order to work through the pain? Write as many as you can in the outer circle.

---

[51] Introduction to BIRTHING FROM WITHIN Workshop Workbook for Mentors and Doulas ©2000-2010

Resilience

For this segment, you will need clay. You can use earth clay or synthetic clay for this activity.

The pliability of clay is a metaphor for the way you can stretch, bend, expand, and contract in birth. Its flexibility parallels your ability to do what works until it doesn't, and then changes shape to do something else. For this birth art assignment, you'll be exploring the concept of resilience.

Take a ball of clay in your hands. Work it with your fingers and allow yourself to become curious about the shape, symbol, or figure that will emerge to represent resilience. The form it takes may be literal or abstract. Continue to add details, features, and ideas to your sculpture until you feel like it captures the concept of resilience.

Set your sculpture down and look at it from a different angle. What do you notice now that you didn't before? What does this symbol tell you about birth?

Now take that sculpture in your hands and bring it back to a ball of clay.[52] This is neither punishment nor cruelty. It is simply an acknowledgment that the landscape of birth is always changing. Sometimes an idea, a way of coping, a mantra, a movement, or a technique can seem like the ultimate coping solution in labor – until it's not. Perhaps the baby changes position, the labor progresses, or something shifts in the environment, and you must find a new way forward.

This is your opportunity to practice the art of perseverance. It may feel annoying or disappointing to crush your sculpture. That's ok. Stay curious about your emotions, the response in your body, and your thoughts. Allow the next sculpture to show itself to you as you work the clay in your hands once more. Give your whole heart to your process, knowing that you will probably have to smash it again. It's still worthwhile to give your full attention and effort to this task. Keep going until it's complete. You are actively practicing resilience.

Examine, journal, smash, repeat – until you discover something new, until you learn something about yourself or about birth that you could not have learned in any other way. There is no way to know if this will require you to smash your sculpture once or sixteen times. That doesn't matter right now. The only thing that matters is how you give all of your heart and attention to this moment.

Through this process, you have witnessed your own creativity and perseverance. You have connected with your ability to access your vast inner resources. You have practiced unattachment to outcome. You have lived the experience of allowing your process to ebb and flow, without it needing to be constantly moving forward in a way that is measurable or straightforward.

---

[52] Pam England, CNM, MA, *Ancient Map for Modern Birth: Preparation, Passage, and Personal Growth during Your Childbearing Year* (Albuquerque: Seven Gates Media, 2017)

What have you learned about yourself through this birth art practice? What have you learned about birth? Who are you when you have to change plans? What do you do when you don't know what to do?

3rd Trimester Ceremony

There is power in connecting with a supportive community and creating a space that is focused on the pregnant parent, their support system, their preparation, and their transformation. More and more modern parents are replacing traditional baby showers with a ceremony that is commonly known as a "Mother Blessing" or "Birth Blessing."

Rather than focusing on gifts for the baby, this type of gathering consists of rituals that help you feel more connected to yourself, your circle, and your passage into parenthood. By the end of the ceremony, you should feel held by a caring community because you have experienced it repeatedly through a series of rituals, which might include:

- A foot bath
- Henna on the belly or hands
- Massage and loving touch
- Bringing a bead to be strung on a bracelet or necklace, representing the support of the participants in the ceremony
- Mindful sharing of stories about birth (see chapter on Birth Stories)
- Prayers or blessings for you and baby
- Acknowledging ancestors
- Drumming

- Dancing
- Creating a quilt of loving and supportive words and symbols for you. Each person could bring one square in a standard size to contribute.
- Gifts for your postpartum adjustment or healing
- Sharing food
- Other traditions that are passed down through your family, culture, or religion

A ceremony to bless you as a pregnant parent is a beautiful way for you to receive nurturing as you prepare to nurture a new life. Some people will even hold an intimate blessing event in addition to the baby shower. What sort of rituals might help you feel more connected to those around you as you prepare for birth? Ask a friend or family member to help you plan a ceremony to celebrate your journey into parenthood.

Welcoming Rituals

Most adults are familiar with the opening scene of *The Lion King* when the whole animal kingdom partakes in a ceremony to welcome the new lion prince. The rituals, the support of close loved ones, and the rejoicing of the whole animal kingdom are very touching to watch. There is beauty in celebrating a new life within a community, in performing special rites to welcome them into your family, and into the world.

When a Muslim baby is first born, their parent will traditionally recite the call to prayer in their right ear. With this ritual comes the hope that the child will respond readily to this call throughout their life.[53]

In Jamaica, the umbilical cord and placenta are buried after birth. A tree is brought by friends or family members to be planted above it. As the child grows older, they learn responsibility by taking care of their special tree.[54]

---

[53] Abu Dawud V.5 Pg.518 Darul Yusr

[54] BellyBelly Staff Writer, "10 Birth Rituals Around the World" (blog) BellyBelly (June 10, 2018) **https://www.bellybelly.com.au/birth/birth-rituals-around-the-world/**

Sikh families will bring their baby to the temple shortly after birth. The priest will open the holy book, the Guru Granth Sahib, to a random page to read aloud. The parents will choose a name for the baby that starts with the first letter of the hymn on that page.[55]

People from the Bassa tribe of Liberia tie a beaded string around the new baby's waist early on in order to help them track the baby's growth. As the rope gets tighter, it helps reassure the parents that the baby is growing well.[56]

It is a beautiful practice to welcome a baby into a community mindfully. If your family or community doesn't have any particular traditions around this special life event, you can create your own. How would you like to greet the newest member of your family and community in a ceremonial way?

---

[55] *Sikhism: Baby Rites*, BBC, 27 Oct. 2009,
https://www.bbc.co.uk/religion/religions/sikhism/ritesrituals/babyrites.shtml

[56] Lisette Austin, "Welcoming Baby: Birth rituals provide children with sense of community, culture" (blog) ParentMap (May 21, 2005) **https://www.parentmap.com/article/welcoming-baby-birth-rituals-provide-children-with-sense-of-community-culture**

Gate of Relief and Gratitude

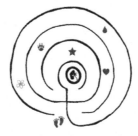

Hopefully the emergence of your little one brings respite and relief from the intensity of labor. In the case of complications with your or the baby's health, this response may be delayed. Typically, gratitude that contractions have ended and that the baby has arrived are the prominent emotions that fill the delivery room just after birth.

For hours, or sometimes days, the birth giver stays suspended in this space of joy and relief. This is a time to soak in your baby, to bask in their newness, and to allow yourself to be awed by all that was involved in their arrival. When you have a few moments, journal about your memories of the birth. Anchor your reflections while they are fresh in your mind at the Gate of Relief and Gratitude[57].

What was a moment when you felt really supported during the birth?

---

[57] Introduction to BIRTHING FROM WITHIN Workshop Workbook for Mentors and Doulas ©2000-2010

What did you do that amazed you, that you didn't realize you could do?

What is your strongest memory of the birth?

What was it like when you met your baby for the first time?

Describe your baby.

What do you want to always remember about the birth, or about these first moments?

Arrival

The term "Golden Hour" describes the period just after birth when you and your baby are left relatively undisturbed to connect with one another. This early period is an opportunity for parents and babies to adjust after the birth, without rushing into weighing, testing, and postpartum procedures that could certainly wait if there's no emergency.

The Golden Hour carries an aura of a glowing, magical time that isn't always realistic for every family. Some parents may even feel like the bond between themselves and the baby has been permanently affected by the Golden Hour being less than golden.

For some birth givers, the hour after birth will be a time of relief that labor is over and amazement in discovering their baby for the first time. For others, there will be lingering pain. Some will have excessive bleeding or shaking. After a cesarean birth, parents will need to have an incision closed. There are many things that can delay the time when parents can give their full attention to enjoying the new life that came into the world. The same is true if there is any kind of issue with the baby's transition or health.

These parents need to have a bridge between the time of the birth and the time when they can really take in the newness of their little one, whether that bridge needs to span minutes or weeks. Let's explore some ways that you can stay connected to the best of your ability if there is a delay in greeting your baby after the birth.

If you have a challenging transition in the immediate postpartum period, the best thing you can do is focus on your own wellbeing. The baby may be able to lie skin-to-skin on your chest while you focus on getting through this time, or the baby may need to be with another parent or caregiver. You can focus on your own coping and health, knowing that tending to your own needs will help ensure your safety and allow you to be present for the baby later, when you are more stable.

What do you suppose you might need *from yourself* if you were having a hard time after the birth? Patience? Gentleness? Something else? Write down words or symbols to portray how your Parent archetype could show up on *your* behalf if the immediate postpartum time is particularly difficult.

When the baby has a health challenge after birth, parents can experience understandable feelings of sadness and regret. It's never easy to watch a child go through health issues, but it is still possible to connect with your baby during health struggles or separations, which could look like…

- Gazing at a photo of your baby while you're pumping milk to give them in the NICU.
- Holding baby skin-to-skin whenever possible.
- Talking to your baby even if you can't hold them. Remember, your voice will be familiar to them.

- Praying for your baby.
- Leaning on others for practical and emotional support when you're struggling. Your baby doesn't just need you, but also the people in your support system. Accepting help will give your baby an early initiation into what it means to belong to a community.

Postpartum Gate of Holy Terror

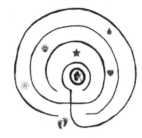

After a brief rest cocooned in the center of the labyrinth, you must turn around and pass through the same gates you traversed to get to the center. Naturally, this makes the Gate of Holy Terror[58] one of the first *postpartum* gates. Entering into postpartum with this awareness doesn't necessarily diminish the amount of overwhelm or uncertainty that you will experience.

It does, however, allow you to navigate this stage with the perspective that it is normal for these emotions to be peppered throughout the first forty days after birth. This knowing can make your experience less isolating and will help prevent feelings of failure or inadequacy.

When you think about the Postpartum Gate of Holy Terror, what do you imagine happening at the most intense moments? Fighting with your partner? Crying? Wanting to give up? Something else?

---

[58] Pam England, CNM, MA, *Ancient Map for Modern Birth: Preparation, Passage, and Personal Growth during Your Childbearing Year* (Albuquerque: Seven Gates Media, 2017)

What is one small thing you could do to cope in that scenario – not that it would take away the situation, but perhaps relieve just a bit of pressure in a really tough moment?

What else might you do for yourself?

Who could you reach out to for help? What might get in the way of you reaching out? Is this an internal obstacle or an external obstacle? What could you do to remove that obstacle?

Physical Healing

In Morocco, it is said that when someone gives birth, their grave is open for forty days.[59] The need for rest and care during this time cannot be overstated. You will need emotional nourishment, love, and support. You will also need to help your body physically recover from the effects of childbirth.

Whether you've been through the postpartum adjustment before or not, what is your sense of what your body will need? What do you suspect will be necessary or helpful for a body that is sore and bleeding? What do you think will be most helpful for residual pain and fatigue? What do you already know about taking care of a depleted body? Write as much as you can below.

---

[59] Layla B., "The Nafsa (new mothers) Grave is Open for 40 Days!! So let's listen up!" (blog) Layla B. (April 3, 2018) **https://www.laylab.co.uk/tnp-blog/open-grave-for-40-days**

Talk to other parents in your social circles about what was most helpful for them in their physical recovery. What do they know now that they wish they had known before giving birth? What one thing made the biggest difference for them? What was least helpful?

After listening to the insights and reflections from others, what more do you need to do to prepare for your postpartum period? Are there resources you need to line up for yourself in advance? Is there something you need to learn, either from a book or your birth attendant? In all of your hunting and gathering about healing physically from birth, what one thing do you suspect will be most impactful for you as you give yourself time, space, and permission to allow your body to heal?

Remembering Self

In the haze of interrupted sleep and the constant adjustments that come with having a new baby, it's easy to lose yourself in a pile of laundry or a 3 am feeding. While many people tell parents that they will never sleep or do the things they enjoy again, this is not true. Becoming a parent doesn't mean that you cease to be the person you were before the birth. It's important to hold on to the things that you love, that fill your cup, and that help you feel whole.

It's true that your time is more limited once you become a parent. It may require some modification or creativity in order to partake in your favorite activities. If you enjoy playing golf, that may mean spending an hour at the driving range instead of playing 18 holes. If you like to run marathons, that may mean getting in a couple miles while the baby naps (once you're done with your initial healing phase).

If you're not deliberate with your free time, it can easily get eaten up by trying to decide what to do, or by non-restorative activities like social media. It will take intention and teamwork to help you connect with the pieces of yourself that feel like coming home. Consider what you could do if you had two hours to yourself. What about one hour? Twenty minutes? Perhaps you would take a bath, read, call a friend, or take the dog for a walk. Write down as many things as you can think of, then come back to this list whenever you can create that time for yourself.

2 hours:

1 hour:

30 minutes:

15 minutes:

Challenges

The time after birth can be a period of sweetness and bonding, but there are also complications that can occur: with your or baby's health, with feeding your baby, and with family adjustments. If you have found yourself in an especially challenging postpartum transition, the journaling prompts below can provide a place to lay your burdens down and offer yourself kindness on this difficult road.

What has helped you cope through this challenge or these challenges? What are the external and internal resources that have supported you along the way?

When did you know you were going to be ok? When did you know that the baby was going to be ok?

What do you know now that you didn't know, and couldn't have known, before?

If you were to tell your baby the story of this time in your lives, what would you want to share with them? What would you want to be understood?

What do you need now – from your partner, your family, your community, and yourself? Is there anything standing in the way of you asking for it? What do you suppose could be done to push beyond these limitations and get the support you need and deserve?

Emotional Healing

There are three components of the Heroic Journey that are an essential part of healing from the emotional impact of your birth: The Unconscious Conditioning, The One Forbidden Thing, and the Call to Return.[60] This constellation of the past, the present, and the future can align to help you change your relationship with the hardest parts of your birth story, and get in touch with your true, essential self in a loving and compassionate way.

You can begin your excavation with the One Forbidden Thing[61] – getting clarity on a moment when you did something that you now feel regretful about, or a moment when something happened externally that made you feel powerless. While there may be multiple moments like this in your birth, find the one that weighs heaviest on your heart today. You can always complete this exploration about another moment at a later time.

---

[60] Joseph Campbell, *The Hero with a Thousand Faces (The Collected Works of Joseph Campbell)* (New World Library, 3rd Edition 2008)

[61] Episode 2 – "The Message of the Myth," Joseph Campbell and the Power of Myth (May 30, 1988) Public Affairs Television and Alvin H. Permutter, Inc. ©

What is a part of your birth that you're struggling to reconcile? A part that makes you feel confused, angry, sad, or disappointed? Narrow it down to just one moment, one scene in the film reel of your birth. Draw a simple picture of this moment below:

Notice the meaning that you are giving this moment. What are you telling yourself that it means about you? What is your internal dialogue now when you look back on this moment? About yourself, or about the other people in the room? About what you did or did not do or say? Notice the competing voices in your mind – how they contradict one another, how the compass of blame sometimes points to one person or another, or even yourself. Write below about your internal dialogue, and your belief about yourself.

Rise up above this scene like a soaring hawk. As the landscape becomes more vast and clear, your perspective expands. Notice the seeds that were watered about the One Forbidden Thing long before you ever became pregnant. Allow other threshold moments to come into your awareness that laid the groundwork for you to feel powerlessness or self-judgment about this moment.

Notice the old, ingrained beliefs from your Unconscious Conditioning about birth, pain, relationships, authority figures, and asking for help that created the framework for you to suppress or judge this part of yourself. What was that early seed that made *this* action, *this* moment, unacceptable in your eyes? As you bring the unconscious to consciousness, journal about what you see in this landscape of your life.

Tune in to the positive intention you had when that belief was created. Were you trying to avoid a punishment? Stay out of trouble? Feel a sense of belonging? What was the basic need that you were trying to meet when you learned or decided that this part of yourself was unacceptable?

Bring your attention back now to the moment of the One Forbidden Thing. When you can connect with your positive intention and your basic human needs, what changes about the way you see yourself in this moment? What shifts in your internal dialogue when you connect this moment with your whole life and everything you ever learned about who you should be, or what you must do in order to get along in the world?

Finally, allow yourself to turn your ear toward The Call to Return. One of the keys to completing the Return, and finding compassion in your birth story, is integrating the One Forbidden Thing. By giving loving kindness to the silenced and suppressed parts of yourself, you begin to change your relationship with a belief that no longer serves you.

If you were to truly accept this part of yourself wholeheartedly, what could you say, or do, or be in your everyday life that would give you more freedom? That would allow you to live something that had not yet been lived, or had not been lived in a very long time? If the One Forbidden Thing were no longer creating invisible barriers within you, blocking you from personal freedom, blocking you from accessing your most authentic self, what might be the first small step you would take?

Collective Story

No birth story stands alone. Each and every birth is a thread in the tapestry of birth in this time and place[62]. When a parent gives birth, the things that they are drawn to or repelled by are determined by a lifetime of stories, patterns, relationships, and conditioning. Partners are also followed by a long train of experiences and learning that informs the way they think, what they do, and what they say.

The beliefs a birth attendant holds about childbirth, pain, hospitals, birthing people, partners, and medicine are all influenced by their education, training, and every birth they have ever witnessed. The same goes for doulas, nurses, and other support people.

Every time a baby is born, their birth story is part of the collective story of birth. Their birth would not have looked the same way on another continent. It would not have looked the same way twenty-five years in the past, or twenty-five years in the future.

---

[62] Pam England, founder of Birthing From Within and Birth Story Medicine. "Birth Story Medicine" course, November 2013, **www.BirthStoryMedicine.com**

Many people view an individual birth like a flower in a vase, examining the petals and leaves – perhaps approving of or judging the actions of the parents. They may evaluate whether or not the parents made "good choices" or "bad choices," and compare their own beliefs about birth to what unfolded during this baby's journey earthside.

To only gaze upon a flower in a vase removes any sense of the system in which that flower bloomed…the soil it grew from, how much sunshine it received, the other flowers and plants it was surrounded by, and the amount of rainwater it absorbed[63]. If we are to look at birth from a holistic perspective, then we must acknowledge the birthing person and everyone who is present at the birth as members of a larger system. This is how we nurture an empathetic understanding of the people and the beliefs, patterns, and emotions that show up in birth.

---

[63] Pam England, founder of Birthing From Within and Birth Story Medicine. "Birth Story Medicine" course, November 2013, **www.BirthStoryMedicine.com**

Becoming a Mentor

When a hero has traversed the unknown and undergone personal transformation, they hear a call to return[64] to their community with the "medicine" of wisdom. In order to become an effective mentor to others, one must walk the path of self-compassion. The wounded storyteller must foster a love for all parts of themselves – the parts that triumphed during the childbearing year, and also the parts of themselves that cracked and crumbled, that cried out in pain, and said "yes" to things that they didn't necessarily want.

The prideful storyteller must love the parts of themselves that could have had a less-than-ideal experience, the parts of themselves that have been judged as weak, whiny, or unworthy by their inner critic. It is only through a commitment to *continuously* work toward self-acceptance that one can fully accept other parents in their journeys and share wisdom from a place of humility. When you find yourself sharing part of your story, ask yourself…

---

[64] Pam England, CNM, MA, *Ancient Map for Modern Birth: Preparation, Passage, and Personal Growth during Your Childbearing Year* (Albuquerque: Seven Gates Media, 2017)

- Is this advice coming from a place of self-judgment?
- Is this story helpful to share?
- Am I trying to convince them to birth in a particular way?
- Does the part of my story that I'm about to share feel unresolved?

When a person has had the resources, introspection, and perhaps mentorship to heal and integrate their birth story, they are ready to bring medicine to their community. The stories they share are about their personal growth, their work in self-compassion, and their process of initiation, rather than the specific details of their birth.

They can become a mentor to others when they share their story, not from a place of needing to be heard, but from a place of no attachment. Forgiveness and self-acceptance echo throughout their story as they share what they learned about themselves along the way. Their story doesn't carry warnings or judgment. It carries unlimited love for themselves and the people they share it with. This is story medicine.

4th Trimester Ceremony

Most cultures mark the postpartum period as lasting for six weeks, or forty days. This is an important time for rest and nurturing. This is a time for parents to be cocooned with support – ideally by a loving family and community – but also by one another.

Together, you and your partner have moved through sleepless nights, the strain of healing, the weight that stress puts on a relationship, and witnessing one another's adjustment into a brand-new role in life. While the challenges of raising your baby certainly aren't over, it's likely that this time marks a gate into a less stressful part of your baby's first year. Perhaps you're getting just a little more sleep, or you're getting the hang of feeding your baby. If not, take heart. Know that easier times are coming, even if the hard days feel like they will last forever.

In Mexico and Morocco, there are ceremonies at the end of the fourth trimester to "close the bones" of the birth giver with a traditional cloth.[65] This is an embodied acknowledgment that the time of gestation has ended, and a signal that parents can close that chapter in their lives with reverence and gratitude for the many facets of their pregnancy journey.

---

[65] Layla B. "Closing the Bones (الشّد - Al Shedd), the Moroccan Way!" (blog) Layla B. June 26, 2018 **https://www.laylab.co.uk/tnp-blog/moroccanclosingthebones**

Tema Mercado, "Postpartum Sealing" La Matriz Birth **http://www.lamatrizbirth.com/postpartum-sealing/**

What traditions does your culture have around marking the end of this period? If a family member doesn't know, then you might research those traditions or discuss this topic with wise elders.

This is a good time to gather your community around you, to care for you and witness your birth as a parent. It may even be a time for sharing gratitude for those who have helped to take care of your family over the last six weeks.

What is your strongest memory from the first 40 days?

What was a big challenge that you (and perhaps your partner and support system) overcame?

How did you manage to do that?

How did you keep going during the hardest times?

How is your baby different now than the first day you welcomed them into your family?

If you were going to offer yourself advice on the first day of parenting, what would it be?

What advice do you suppose you would offer your current self one year from now?

Dearest Reader,

Thank you for embarking on this journey of self-discovery with me. Thank you for your vulnerability, determination, and willingness to explore your inner world. May you experience the power of deep self-compassion in birth and postpartum. May you be well-supported on your Heroic Journey. May you know the unconditional love that you deserve, now and always.

All my love,

Nikki Shaheed

Resources

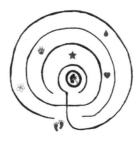

Do you want to continue to explore these concepts with a supportive community? Join the Heart Centered Pregnancy Facebook group to connect with other parents who are on a journey toward self-knowing at
https://www.facebook.com/groups/2690399274336382/

If you are a parent who wants to receive personal mentoring, childbirth education, or doula support from a Birthing From Within professional, please visit **www.BirthingFromWithin.com** to find a practitioner in your area.

If you are a birth professional who feels inspired by this book, please join us at one of our in-person or online trainings to help you deepen your practice and connect with parents on a whole new level.

Please consider leaving a review of this journal on Amazon to help other parents.

Made in the USA
Coppell, TX
23 April 2020